Jailbirds &
Stool Pigeons

Jailbirds & Stool Pigeons
Crime Stories of the West

by Norman L. Davis

hancock
house

ISBN 0-88839-431-4
Copyright © 1999 Norman L. Davis

Cataloging in Publication Data
Davis, Norman, 1933-
  Jailbirds and stool pigeons

  Includes bibliographical references.
  ISBN 0-88839-431-4

  1. Prisons--West (U.S.)--Anecdotes. 2. Outlaws--West
(U.S.)--Biography. 3. Prisons--Northwest, Pacific--Anecdotes.
4. Outlaws--Northwest, Pacific--Biography. 5. West (U.S.)--
History--1890-1945. 6. Northwest, Pacific--History. I. Title.
HV9475.W38D38 1999   365'.978   C98-911162-8

Editor: Nancy Miller
Production: Ingrid Luters and Nancy Miller
Cover design: Ingrid Luters
Cover photos: Utah State Prison *courtesy of Utah State Historical Society*
            Tom McCarty (inset) *courtesy of Utah State Archives*

Published simultaneously in Canada and the United States by

HANCOCK HOUSE PUBLISHERS LTD.
19313 Zero Avenue, Surrey, B.C. V4P 1M7
(604) 538-1114 Fax (604) 538-2262

HANCOCK HOUSE PUBLISHERS
1431 Harrison Avenue, Blaine, WA 98230-5005
(604) 538-1114 Fax (604) 538-2262
Web Site: www.hancockhouse.com *email:* sales@hancockhouse.com

Contents

Preface

I wrote these stories to relate the facts as the participants' contemporaries recorded them. Too often, partial truths become legend and are eventually accepted as fact. For example, Wyatt Earp, contrary to popular belief, was never a U.S. marshall or even a deputy marshall. And he never owned a Colt "Buntline Special" revolver.

In an effort to put people straight, I wrote about Bill Miner, the subject of the totally false movie, *The Grey Fox*. In doing research for that book, I came across other interesting stories that are fact and fascinate. My sources were prison records, U.S. census, state and county records, contemporary newspapers and some manuscripts. Sometimes I would find conflicting reports and had to use discretion in choosing what I thought were the true facts. At times, there are pieces of information missing, such as people's first names, or there are gaps of time between elements of a story. Rather than speculate, I have put down what I know to be true, no more and no less. If one were to read *Last of the Bandit Riders* by Matt Warner and *The Outlaw Trail* by Charles Kelly and my story on the McCarty clan, I suspect mine would be accepted more so than the others.

Let the readers be the judge and deliberate.

The Life and Times of the McCarty Gang

This is the story of an outlaw family—the McCartys. They were John (Tom) Thomas; William (Billy) A.; George (Craps) W.; Billy's son Fred (Kid); George's wife Albina (Nellie) McCarty, she was also called Sparta, Queen of the Forest; and Erastus Christiansen, known both as Matt Warner and Diamond Dick, brother-in-law of Tom McCarty.

Their father was Dr. Alexander G. McCarty known as a successful good doctor and farmer. Their sister Lois married Hank Vaughn, a charming horse thief, murderer and gunfighter. He was known to have thirteen bullet wounds on various parts of his body. Billy's stepson Eck, working as a waiter, killed a customer with a corkscrew and was acquitted in court.

Tom and Billy mentored Robert LeRoy Parker, also known as Butch Cassidy, into a life of rustling and robberies. Tom was credited with perfecting the art of the getaway by using stolen horses picked for speed and endurance. The horses then were secreted at strategic intervals and used as relays. Tom was always the leader, but always held the horses except for the Wilcox, Wyoming, robbery. Tom was the very active leader at Wilcox. No posse ever caught Tom or his crime partners riding away on horseback.

At sixty-three years of age, Tom went to prison for stealing less than twenty dollars from a drunk. By then he had become a hopeless alcoholic himself. He drowned himself on the thirty-third anniversary of his brother and nephew's death during a bank robbery that went bad for all concerned. Here is their story.

Ringgold County in southwestern Iowa was a primitive prairie in 1853. The soil was rich and elk and buffalo fed on its luxuriant grasses. Mt. Ayr was founded and three miles southwest in Rice township Doctor Alexander G. and Mary Ann Palmer McCarty located a farm. They had started married life together in Brown County, Indiana. Their son John Thomas was born there late in 1850 at Mt. Moriah. He was forever known as Tom. William A. was born in Iowa in 1852 and was called Billy. In 1856 Lois was born; in 1859 Laura arrived but died in early childhood. George was born in Des Moines on May 10, 1862.

Mt. Ayr was less than twenty miles from Missouri and border gangs started raiding early in the Civil War. Southern sympathizers would raid northern sympathizers and would be retaliated against in kind. The family moved to the safety of Des Moines and then in 1864 moved to Montana. Daughter Rosa was born there and then the family moved to Utah. Reatha was born in Salt Lake City on September 18, 1872. The doctor bought forty-four acres for $63 in the village of Chicken Creek in December, 1871. Chicken Creek is about three miles southwest of Levan in Juab County. The family operated Painted Rocks Horse Ranch there.

Tom and Billy squatted in Grass Valley in the summer of 1873. They claimed all the land from the north end of modern Otter Creek Reservoir south to Antimony. They never legally registered their claim and made life difficult for other settlers by warning them away. They rustled stock and pastured them till they drove them to Colorado where they were sold to hungry miners. A beef in Beaver went for $10, but in Colorado it could fetch $25. Other rustlers joined them, and in 1876 the population of McCarty Rancho was twenty-five.

During December of 1873 four young Navajos were en route to their village after trading in Cache Valley. A snow storm forced them to camp for four days on McCarty land. They killed a calf to eat. En route again they stopped at the McCarty cabin just as Tom and Billy were cooking breakfast. The Natives walked in and before the language barrier was overcome hostile attitudes prevailed. Tom and Billy were forced from the cabin and the Indians ate their breakfast. As the newcomers ate, the brothers tied a bundle of hay with a rope and rolled it at the cabin. The Indians ran out and two were killed and two mounted horses racing away. They were pursued to Center Creek where one was killed and the other wounded. The wounded Indian ran down Black Canyon and hid in the willows. He treated the wound in his side with a poultice of tree bark and prickly pear cactus. He began a twenty-one-day journey home, part of which included a swim in the ice-cold Colorado River in January.

The McCartys took possession of the Indians' trade goods. They had eleven horses, two buffalo robes, two black and red blankets, two buckskins, seven Navajo saddles, three bridles, four quivers full of arrows, one bow and one rifle.

Most settlers left the valley to avoid the Indians seeking vengeance. Brigham Young, the Mormon leader, heard about the incident and sent word to Jacob Hamblin to use his influence to avoid an Indian war. In 1870 Hamblin had been able to convinced the Navajos to make peace ending a three-year war and live and trade with the Mormons in harmony. Young was hoping Hamblin could be a help in settling this dispute.

Hamblin left his sick bed and rode to Lees Ferry where the Smith brothers agreed to accompany him. No one else volunteered to escort him as they feared the Navajos would kill them. On January 29, 1874, the group encountered the Navajos at Moencoppy Wash and rode to their village. The talks began with the wounded Indian demanding that the whites be killed. Others demanded payment of 350 head of horses and cattle. Hamblin said the killers were not Mormons but the McCarty brothers and refused payment. The Navajos threatened to torture Hamblin with fire. Hamblin said he knew no fear and what happened to him was of no consequence but there must be peace. Finally the Indians agreed to meet Hamblin in the spring at the murder scene. There they would determine if the McCartys were guilty and not Mormons.

Jacob Hamblin wrote the following letter on March 10, 1874, to the brothers.

Mr. McCarty

Dear Sir,

I deem it proper to open communication with you concerning the unhappy occurrence of the killing of three and wounding

Top left: John Thomas McCarty, "Tom"
or "Walluke."
Photo: Utah State Historical Society

Above: William "Billy" McCarty.
Photo: Utah State Historical Society

Left: George "Craps" McCarty.
Photo: Mr. & Mrs. Riley

Hank Vaughn. *Photo: Mr. & Mrs. Riley*

Lois, Reatha and Rosa McCarty. *Photo: Mr. & Mrs. Riley*

Lois McCarty Vaughn Hunsaker. *Photo: Mr. & Mrs. Riley*

Albina "Nellie" Blanchett McCarty
"Sparta, Queen of the Forest."
Photo: Mr. & Mrs. Riley

one Navajo at or near your place. I have traveled some eight or nine hundred miles and exerted myself to prevent, if possible, any more bloodshed and settle this unhappy affair.

I have just returned from the Navajo country, where the relatives of the persons killed lived. After the labors and pains I have taken this far, we have come to the conclusion that it would be just and prudent at least for you to forward to the father and the relatives of the Indians killed, the horses and other property they left behind them; or, if you will forward them to me, I will be responsible that the relatives get them. I herewith forward you an account of the before named property, as described by the Navajo....

I saw the wounded Indian a few days since. He is nearly well. The three who were killed had their tickets of leave from the agent at Fort Defiance and were of good character.

I think you would do well to comply in returning the before mentioned property.

(Signed) Jacob Hamblin
Indian Agent
I fully endorse the above.
(Signed) Stewart, Bishop of Kanab
P.S. We want your earliest convenience for an answer.
To Mr. McCarty, Stock Raiser at Circle or Grass Valley, on the Sevier River—Post Master Please Forward

Two hundred Indians became impatient and rode north to avenge the deaths. Issac Riddle met them and convinced them to return to their homes. When the Indians and Hamblin met in the spring, peace was maintained. The Indians were convinced Hamblin was truthful. Many people owed their wellbeing to a brave, dedicated Jacob Hamblin, and also Issac Riddle.

Tom and Billy never returned the property or answered the letter. Undoubtedly Maximillian Parker delivered that letter. Max Parker delivered mail from Beaver to the Sevier River Valley. His son Robert LeRoy Parker, later known as Butch Cassidy, may have ridden along the mail route. The Parkers lived in Circleville at that time.

On January 5, 1875, the highlight of the winter social season in Circleville was the wedding of William A. McCarty and Lettie

Maxwell Brown. It took place at the home of Alexander Maxwell. Lettie had a four-year-old son E. C., who was always called Eck. Perhaps young Robert Parker shared a piece of wedding cake with Eck. Sons Fred and Pearl were born in 1875 and 1878 respectively to the young couple.

Tom married Christina (Teenie) Christiansen about 1873. She was the daughter of Christian and Christina Christiansen who emigrated from Denmark to embrace the Mormon faith. Teenie had three brothers, Neils, Anthony and Erastus. The latter was born in 1864 and had many aliases but was best known as Matt Warner. Tom and Teenie were the parents of Lewis, born in 1874. They then had a son Leonard in 1878 and then Dora in 1880. Teenie died June 21, 1881; Tom then abandoned his children and her parents raised them. Dora died when she was fourteen.

In 1879, Alexander and Mary McCarty made their final move to Myrtle Creek, Oregon, once again establishing his practice in a small town and opening a drug store. There, he donated land for a cemetery and church. George had accompanied his parents to Myrtle Creek and was soon involved with Ruby Cornelison. Abandoning usual Victorian morals, Ruby was six-months pregnant when they married February 13, 1879. Son Claud was born May 15, 1879. No longer enamored of Ruby's company, George joined his brothers in Grass Valley. Soon he was courting Albina "Nellie" Blanchett. She lived with her parents in Marysvale, not far from McCarty Rancho. George and Nellie married in Ogden, Utah, August 24, 1884.

The McCartys overstocked the range with their stolen cattle. Then in 1879 a severe drought forced them to move southeast of Moab. About one mile northwest of Old La Sal Post Office on Coyote Creek, they and relatives built homes, barns and corrals. Billy had 2,000 head of cattle. Philander Maxwell, Billy's brother-in-law, and the Rays and Taylors enjoyed some good years.

During August of 1883 the families enjoyed a horse race. Billy bet $1,000 and twenty head of horses on his horse Selim who ran against Tobe, owned by the Rays. Tobe won easily. Neal Ray offered to race another horse whose jockey weighed 165 pounds. Eck weighed 105 pounds, thus enjoying a sixty-pound

13

Gravestones of Dr. Alexander McCarty, Dec. 8, 1825 – Nov. 26, 1894, and Mary Ann Palmer McCarty, Jan. 27, 1830 – October 9, 1913, Myrtle Creek, Douglas County, Oregon.

Photo: Norman Davis

Dr. Alexander G. McCarty donated the land this church was built on. His grandson Claud helped construct it.

Photo: Norman Davis

Parade in Moab, Utah circa 1900.

Photo: Utah State Historical Society

Tom carved his name on a remote canyon wall near the Colorado River in Utah.

Photo: Utah State Historical Society

advantage. Eck lost by one length. The McCartys were gracious losers and scheduled another race for September. Eck then rode Bally and beat Tobe.

The year 1885 brought mild weather and little in the way of Indian troubles; therefore, the calf crop in the spring of 1885 was very good. Charles H. Ogden and Jim Blood representing the Pittsburgh Cattle Company bought the ranch and stock. Some of Billy's relatives moved to Paradox, Colorado, just across the state line. (This information is found in *History and Settlement of Northern San Juan County* by Frank Silvey. However, none of the names appear in the grantee/grantor index in the 1880s. It is probable then that the Pittsburgh Cattle Company just bought stock but no land as it wasn't registered at the court house in Monticello.) Apparently Billy and company just squatted on the land as they had in Grass Valley.

Tom rustled, raced horses, gambled and robbed stagecoaches. Always on the move, he returned to Mt. Ayr for a visit. There he bought three horses and shipped them west on the railroad.

Most outlaws have a Robin Hood story somewhere in their legend. Tom related one in his autobiography that is vaguely verified in local folklore. The probable location was on the Mormon Trail in southwestern Utah.

Antelope Springs was a stagecoach station with a large barn, dance hall and saloon next to the Williams Hotel. The stagecoaches were known to carry gold bars from the mines in DeLaMar east to Salt Lake City. Tom arrived there one evening hoping to get a good supper. Since he was wanted for rustling and stage coach robberies, he approached cautiously walking the last mile on foot. He hid when the stagecoach arrived and the passengers were called to supper. A lady passenger asked a man to assist her in negotiating the long step from the coach by holding her baby momentarily. He rudely refused saying that he wasn't a baby handler. He was a large overweight man with eye glasses and a stovepipe hat. Tom decided to teach the man some manners.

16

Tom rode about three miles from the station locating a good holdup spot. In due time the coach arrived and he stepped into the road shouting "hands up." Tom ordered the passengers to dismount and took $300 from a doctor. The rude man pleaded for Tom not to shoot and was relieved of his valuables. A miner didn't have enough to steal but the lady offered her purse with $2.35 in it. Tom put three $20 bills in it and returned it to her. Tom then took the stovepipe hat and glasses from the rude man and made him apologize to the lady. Then he made the man walk back to Antelope Springs. Some of this story is probably true.

Billy moved his family to eastern Oregon. One R. C. George sold 360 acres to Billy on June 29, 1885, for $4,050 cash money paid in hand and receipt issued. The land was about twelve miles north of Baker and east of Haines. It was within a mile of where the Oregon Trail and the forty-fifth parallel cross. (The forty-fifth parallel is halfway between the equator and the North Pole.)

Billy bought cattle and was thought to have adequate finances. He was a spendthrift but sometimes drank heavily. During these binges he would "buck the tiger," that is, play faro. He lost $10,000 at one faro bank and also lost at poker. In 1890, he drove several hundred head of cattle to the Big Bend area of central Washington for winter grazing. During the following brutal winter he lost the herd.

George and Nellie also moved to eastern Oregon locating on Cracker Creek. Later the name was changed to Bourne. George began placer mining and prospecting. Bourne was in a very narrow, steep canyon but produced millions in gold. It boasted of twenty saloons, one store and a livery stable.

Lois McCarty married Hank Vaughn soon after his release from Oregon State Prison. Hank located in Kelton, Utah, and made his living as a blacksmith, a trade he had learned in prison. In appearance he resembled a clergyman. He always wore black suits, a soft hat and a black tie. He accessorized with gold chains, rings and a fine gold watch. He carried elaborate Colt revolvers. He was a popular, charming and charismatic murderer and bullying drunkard.

His first shooting scrape occurred when he and a partner stole some horses. Sheriff Frank Maddock and deputies from Umatilla County tracked the pair to their camp on the Burnt River. Instead of surrendering upon command, Hank shot the sheriff in his jaw and a deputy was killed. Hank's partner was killed and Hank was wounded. Hank was recovering in jail when a lynch mob appeared. Deputy John Hailey drew his Colt revolvers and compelled the mob to disperse. Hank was sentenced to life on June 14, 1865, when he was fifteen. The governor pardoned him on February 22, 1870.

After marrying Lois, he moved to Elko, Nevada. Lois bore one son and was pregnant with another when Hank deserted her. She returned to her parents in Myrtle Creek. Hank moved to Pendleton, Oregon.

Hank met a man named Long in a saloon and they soon argued violently. To settle their differences they each took hold of a handkerchief and emptied their revolvers into each other. Then they beat one another over the head till they passed out from blood loss. Each had been shot several times, but amazingly they both survived. They became good friends. Soon after recovering Hank met a man named Caldwell in a saloon. Since Caldwell was a stranger he was compelled to dance as Hank fired his revolver into the floor. Caldwell took offense and soon returned armed and shot Hank in his right arm. Hank recovered in bed and amused himself by shooting left handed at a playing card on the wall.

After rejoining her parents, Lois operated a boarding house in Grants Pass, Oregon. Joe Hunsaker was a fireman on the first train into Grants Pass. He soon married Lois and they moved to Baker where he worked in the White Swan Mine. It was a rich mine and worked for years.

Hank married Martha Robey, a woman of Umatilla-white origin with a fine ranch on the Umatilla Indian Reservation. She had five children from a previous marriage. In 1888, quite by chance, Hank met Lois on a street in Pendleton. Each thought the other was dead. Hank retained an attorney and sought a divorce, which was granted. Hank was unaware of the second son.

One day in early June of 1893, Hank left a saloon drunk and galloped his horse recklessly in the streets of Pendleton. The horse couldn't keep up with Hank's demands and it stumbled. Hank was thrown onto some rocks at the railroad grade. He suffered massive head injuries and remained in a coma till he died at 8 p.m. on the fifteenth. Local lawmen confiscated his fine revolvers and retain them to this date at the Oregon State Sheriff Historical Association. There was a large funeral but the widow was too distraught to attend. She never remarried. Since he was dead, people openly discussed how he made his living. He was thought to have been involved with the McCartys dealing in stolen horses and probably robberies.

Some chroniclers of the McCartys hold them responsible for the robbery of the Denver and Rio Grande Railroad just six miles east of Grand Junction, Colorado, in November of 1887. The engineer stopped the train to avoid hitting a pile of ties and rocks on the tracks. Three men pointed revolvers at the crew and all proceeded to the mail car. They took about $100 from registered letters and went to the express car. The clerk refused to open the door and told the bandits he was ignorant of the safe's combination. Frustrated, the bandits rode away. A posse found nothing and soon quit.

The bandits were never positively identified but a $5,400 reward was posted. It is possible it was Tom and Matt and an unknown. They were very familiar with the area. Nearby was the San Miguel River that flows northwesterly to join the Delores River then into the Colorado north of Moab.

High in the mountains of southwestern Colorado was the mining town of Telluride. The San Miguel Valley Bank handled the payrolls for some local mines like the Smuggler, Liberty Bell, Black Bear and the Alta. In planning the robbery, Tom is credited with originating the idea of secreting fresh horses at strategic intervals on the getaway route. That way they could mount fresh horses and drive the tired horses ahead of them. The posse would be unable to catch them on tired horses. Tom and Butch Cassidy used this plan many times and no posse ever caught them. Tom,

Matt and Butch had camped just out of town for several days. They spent their time caring for their fine horses and inquiring about mine payroll arrivals at the bank. They learned that a $24,000 payroll had been delivered to the bank on June 23, 1889.

About 9:30 A.M. of the 24th, the three rode into town and entered a saloon. After enjoying a drink and lighting cigars they casually walked their horses to the bank. Tom remained outside holding the horses. It was late in the morning and some bank employees had gone to lunch. Teller Hyde and San Miguel County Clerk Charles Painter were alone in the bank. Matt and Butch drew their revolvers and demanded money. Hyde quickly handed over about $21,000 and the pair left. Quickly mounting they galloped out of town. Ed Wellen, a local boy, was standing on the boardwalk and Tom fired a shot to scare the youngster.

Sheriff Baty soon organized a posse of twelve men and the chase was on. As the racing bandits reached Wichmann's Brewery, a cowboy recognized all three and joined in the pursuit. Having a fresh horse he quickly caught up to the quarry. Tom rode around a rock and dismounted drawing his revolver. He stopped the cowboy and relieved him of a pearl-handled revolver. Remounting, Tom rode off proving he was not a ruthless killer, except when he met up with Indians.

Soon after, another posse member got very close but suddenly realized that he could not capture all three by himself. He stopped to answer an urgent call of nature. For the rest of his life he was ridiculed for stopping.

The posse was too close for the bandits to stop at their first relay. The dead horses were found months later still tied to a tree. Eventually the bandits outdistanced the posse. A three-way split amounted to more than $7,000 each. They rode through Moab to Robbers Roost where they split up. Then Matt married Rosa and moved to Beasley Springs, Washington. Butch went to Wyoming and Tom went to visit brother Billy in Haines, Oregon.

Billy's stepson Eck was a waiter in the Lyceum Theater in Baker, Oregon. During the evening of November 19, 1890, he served champagne to T. C. Winningham, a local citizen, and his showgirl friends Misses Jennie Riley and Jackie Payton. They were all fond of bubbly so more was ordered and Winningham paid with $20 gold coins. About 11 P.M. Winningham was drunk and demanded his change for several bottles. Eck said he had brought change with each bottle. Winningham turned out his pockets to find only fifty cents. Enraged, Winningham drew a knife and advanced toward Eck who hit him with a corkscrew above his eye. Winningham fell unconscious with a fractured skull. He was taken to jail where he died the next day. He left a widow and five children. Eck was arrested and charged with murder.

The courtroom was packed without even standing room. The testimony and evidence were presented and the jury deliberated twenty-four hours. They returned a not guilty verdict. Lettie hugged her son. Billy wasn't there.

At this time the family (Tom, Billy, George, Fred, Matt and Nellie) formed a gang and planned to rob banks. They took nicknames and Tom was Wahluke. That was the Indian name given to a place on the Columbia River south of Beasley Springs. It meant watering or drinking place, which accurately described Tom's thirst for alcohol. Billy was Firefoot and Matt was Diamond Dick. Fred was Kid, George was Craps and Nellie was Sparta, Queen of the Forest.

About seventy miles north of Haines in Oregon's Wallowa Mountains was the town of Enterprise. W. R. Holmes was the cashier of the Wallowa National Bank. About 1 P.M. of October 8, 1891, Holmes returned from lunch and resumed his place at the counter. He was confronted by a man who inquired if a deposit in the name of Smith had been received from a Portland bank. Holmes replied saying no, but was then faced with two men who drew revolvers and demanded money from the vault. Holmes protested, claiming he was ignorant of the combination. Two revolvers were pressed into his midsection and he was threatened with immediate death. This caused him to open the vault and hand out $3,450 to the bandits. A sack of silver coins was dropped and Holmes was compelled to pick up the money. He

Summerville, Oregon
1890-1900

Bank of Summerville is on the left, the false-fronted building between the two highest buildings.

Photo: unknown

Wallowa National Bank in Enterprise, Oregon. The McCartys robbed this on October 8, 1891, long before this picture was taken in the 1930s. It is open for business as a flower shop currently. It still has four vaults.

Photo: Oregon Historical Society, negative #665-96

was then forced out the door with the bandits. Quickly mounting their horses and galloping south, the bandits fired their revolvers into the air. The mountain passes were closed by snow, so the gang rode around them to Haines. A posse soon gave up and a reward of $500 was offered for the responsibles capture. Since the split was less than $1,000 each, another robbery was planned.

Summerville was even closer to Haines, just forty-five miles north. H. C. Rinehart closed the Summerville Bank on time November 3, 1891. Then it was his habit to answer correspondence and do some bookkeeping. At 9 P.M. he was leaving for home when two men with drawn revolvers forced him back into the bank. They ordered him to open the vault or die. He opened the vault and surrendered $4,800. He was told to remain in the vault and they started to close the door. He protested that he would perish from lack of air before the vault would be opened in the morning. They spared his life and rode into the cold darkness. With this loss and the Panic of 1893, when there was financial collapse in the United States, the bank failed.

The gang enjoyed a comfortable winter planning their next robbery. Their attempt at robbing a train failed miserably. Less than twenty miles from Haines on May 4, 1892, a Union Pacific westbound train approached Tunnel Number 5. This was between North Powder and Telocaset. In the darkness, but illuminated by the train headlight, Engineer Al Stevens saw a man by the track waving a flag. Stevens slowed the train almost to a stop but saw the man had a rifle behind him. Stevens opened the throttle and the train jumped ahead, then Stevens saw the man was masked. The man fired at the engine and the bullet splattered on its boiler plate (sheet steel). The crew saw four more masked men ride away. Conductor Grady saw the events from the baggage car, armed himself and then hurried to the passenger car. The passengers were quickly hiding money and valuables. Grady took a count of passengers who were armed. Too few were armed, and most with small-caliber revolvers. A pursuit on foot in the darkness would be futile. All were relieved when the danger passed.

The next night a sheep camp on the lower Powder River was raided. Five men rode in and stole everything in sight. A team and wagon, camping equipment, food and a tent were taken. The gang was obviously planning a trip.

The following Saturday evening about 8 P.M., five masked men entered the store of E. E. Clough in Sparta. At revolver point they ordered the safe opened. It was and $325 in currency, $135 in gold dust plus a $48-nugget was taken. They also took boots, clothing, food, gold watches and other items. The customers were ordered to march about 100 yards away and stay there. After the bandits left, a messenger was dispatched to Baker for the sheriff. The sheriff sent one deputy to investigate.

Fred McCarty proved there is no honor among thieves. He found the gold hidden in the chicken coop. He took it to Boise, Idaho, and had a fine time spending the gold. The gang traveled to Beasley Springs (later Ephrata) to visit Matt and Rosa who were expecting a baby. Rosa's sister, Sarah Jane Morgan, was helping the mother-to-be. Together they operated a cafe catering to railroad workers. Rosa cooked and Matt did the menial, nasty chores and hated it. Often he would go to Coulee City to gamble. He was a mean drunk and beat Rosa when angered. Once he made Rosa step to the six-gun dance.

Simultaneously, Oregon lawmen were arresting people. During May, Sheriff Boles and deputies arrested R. J. Harris, D. F. Hart and William Wells for the attempted train robbery, Sparta store robbery and the two bank robberies in Enterprise and Summerville. Mrs. Hart presented her jailed husband with a child the next day. She was destitute and was forced to rely on charity for life's necessities. A search of the Harris place revealed stolen property. Freshly made bearskin masks similar to the masks worn by the unsuccessful train robbers were found. James Comstock was arrested for stealing saddles found at the Harris place.

Sheriff Conde of Baker County arrested William Gale and Dick Barclay near the town of John Day in Grant County. They were thought to be the ring leaders. All pled not guilty. They were indicted for robbery and assault while being armed with a dangerous weapon. They secured attorneys but were found guilty by jury trials on May 30. Barclay and Gale were sentenced to fifteen years each. Harris, Hart and Wells each were sentenced to five years. Comstock pled guilty and received three years. All arrived at Oregon State Prison in Salem in early June. Frank Hart was pardoned after serving eight months. Harris was released in 1894. Wells and Comstock were released in 1895. Gale and Barclay served more than ten years being released Christmas week of 1902.

About eighty miles east of Seattle, Washington, near the eastern entrance of Snoqualmie Pass is the coal mining town of Roslyn. The Northern Pacific Coal Company owned the mine and store. Ben E. Snipes owned the bank. At 5 A.M. on Saturday, September 24, 1892, three of the gang watched the $40,000 mine payroll being transferred from the Northern Pacific Express car at Cle Elum station to the coach car on the Roslyn Branch Line. Then they rode the few miles to Roslyn and waited in a saloon across the street from the bank. It was a low overcast, foggy, rainy day. They all had a drink to ward off the chill. As they enjoyed good spirits they failed to see the paymaster pick up the payroll and return to the company office. It was payday and the paymaster prepared pay envelopes. Miners off shift were loitering in the streets awaiting pay call.

A few minutes after 2 P.M. five armed men went to the bank. Tom and George held the horses while Billy, Fred and Matt entered. They demanded money at gunpoint. Cashier Abernathy had a revolver close to hand and Matt saw him reach for it. He hit Abernathy a stunning blow to his head and he fell bleeding to the floor. He stayed there while Fred emptied the safe of currency into a sack. Dr. Lyon, who had been doing some banking, knelt to treat Abernathy's wound. The bandits were mounting as F. A. Frazier, an assistant cashier, was returning from an errand. Frazier quickly interpreted the situation and secured a shotgun. As he advanced menacingly, Tom shot him in his hip. A black man also approached and Tom shot him in his leg. The robbers then raced north out of town.

In the foggy fading daylight and occasional rain showers, the robbers raced past the side trail where Nellie waited with the relay horses. Finally they realized their error and reversed course till they found it. Quickly saddling the fresh horses they drove the tired ones ahead of them. In doing so, they failed to see the tracks of the posse ahead of them. The posse had passed them while they resaddled. The group rode on to the Teanaway Bridge where the posse had stopped.

A posse member shouted "halt" and was answered by gunfire. The gang swerved off the road and went up brushy hillsides on wet, slippery rocks. Darkness was their salvation and the posse never saw them again. Either during the exchange of gunfire or while resaddling Fred dropped his revolver and shot himself in his leg. Nellie accompanied him to Haines by stagecoach and train. Tom, Billy, George and Matt rode easterly mostly at night. They became lost but encountered Ole Hanson, a local farmer, who agreed to guide them to the Columbia River for ten dollars. Arriving on the bank, Matt started to hand Ole the ten dollars but dropped it. Ole bent to pick it up and Matt hit him with his revolver. They found several boats but all had strong chains and locks securing them. Finally they found one without oars. They went to a deserted sawmill and finding old boards whittled them into suitable oars. They rowed across the mile-wide river towing the horses. Finally they reached Ephrata and divided the $5,500 into equal shares. They planned to rob a train in two weeks but delayed that till Thanksgiving Day.

Photographs and descriptions of the horses found by the posse were circulated over the northwest. Ben Snipes, president of the bank that was robbed, hired the Thiel Detective Agency to find the culprits. Detective M. C. Sullivan was assigned the case. By the end of November Sullivan had identified several men as the bandits. He organized a twenty-five-man posse in Portland, Oregon. They went east by train to north central Oregon. Cal Hale, Tom Kinzie, George and Willis Thackery, Byron Bernard and Peter Humphrey were arrested. The prisoners were jailed in Kittitas County Jail in Ellensburg, Washington. At a press conference Detective Sullivan said that this was the most desperate gang of outlaws that ever operated in the west. He was proud of his part in their capture. One of the arrested men had a horse branded 7L and Matt Warner's brand was 7U, easy to confuse at a distance. Cashier Abernathy immediately identified Cal Hale as the man who struck him. Dr. Lyon said Kinzie was one of the bandits. Most of the other witnesses weren't sure these were the men responsible. The defendants were granted separate trials. A prosecution witness was sick for a month and delayed the trial till February 1, 1893. Ben Snipes hired at his expense attorney Henry J. Snively to assist prosecutor E. E. Wager.

During the long winter days and nights awaiting trial, Cal Hale wrote this poem.

> On the 24th of September
> All in the present year
> Five bold and dashing highwaymen
> In the town of Roslyn appear.
> They rode straightway to the Roslyn Bank
> And gave these stern commands
> "Gentlemen if you value your life
> Obey, throw up your hands."
> The cashier seemed to hesitate
> Which he should not have done
> As one of the boys reminded him
> By tapping him with his gun.
> They next went over to the safe
> Its contents to unfold
> And took there from $5,000
> In notes and shining gold.
> They then remounted their horses
> Their horses good and true
> And with a few good parting shots
> Bid Roslyn town adieu.
> Excitement at that very time
> In Roslyn town ran high
> And the deputies and detectives
> Were out and on the fly.
> A reward was offered by the bank
> And another by the State
> To arouse those hungry bloodhounds
> And their greed to stimulate.
> They scoured the country all around
> Like school boys out for fun

But not a robber could they find
Nor the way which they had gone.
Then up spoke the meanest cur of all,
And Sullivan is his name,
"This blood-money I must try and get
Likewise I'll get some fame."
So he whistled to his minions
Some five and twenty strong
Saying we'll arrest some of these fellows
Away up in Oregon.
So they arrested five men
Five men both true and good
That never saw the Roslyn Bank
Nor the town in which it stood.
They brought them down to Ellensburg
And threw them into jail
There to await their trial
On 10,000 dollars bail.
Now good people all come join me
When I offer up this prayer
That Sullivan and his bloodhounds
The fires of hell may share.
May they suffer all the tortures
The Devil himself can plan
Is my earnest prayer for Sullivan
And all his cursed clan.

At Cal Hale's trial witnesses Dr. Lyons, Jenkins, Mrs. Clemens and Abernathy identified Hale as one of the bandits. Others only said that he resembled one of the bandits. The prosecution had twelve witnesses and the defense seventeen. They testified as to Hale's good character and established an alibi. The jury deliberated five hours and returned a verdict of guilty.

Thomas A. Kinzie's trial started the seventh of February. This time eye witness identification was less convincing and Kinzie established a credible alibi. The jury deadlocked, seven for acquittal and five guilty. Suddenly all of the accused were freed and Hale given an unconditional release.

Sarah Jane Morgan, Rosa's sister, had written a convincing letter to H. J. Snively of the Bankers Association of Washington declaring the McCartys and Matt Warner were the bank robbers. Sarah developed a hatred for Matt because he abused Rosa. Matt had become enamored of Sarah hoping to establish a polygamous relationship with her and Rosa. Sarah had become engaged to Joe Brooks, Matts' partner in the butcher business. Sarah wanted to return to Salt Lake City but Matt forbade it. Many arguments occurred and finally Sarah said she would inform the law about certain robberies Matt had committed. Matt became furious and threatened to cut off her ears and nose and mutilate her so badly that even a dog would not look at her. He would have beat her but Rosa intervened. Then Matt made her step lively to the six-gun dance. Sarah told Joe Brooks and he took her to Salt Lake City. There she wrote the incriminating letter. She was escorted to Ellensburg and jailed as a material witness.

Deputy Sheriff Banks of Kittitas County and detectives Eaton and Farley arrived in Baker on April third. They had arrest warrants for the McCartys. Farley had previously been chief of police in Denver, Colorado, and was anxious to arrest Tom for a March 29, 1889, robbery of the city's First National Bank. The lawmen called on Sheriff Conde to assist in effecting the arrests.

Sheriff Conde and Deputy Francis went to Billy's ranch east of Haines. Eck told the lawmen that Billy was gone but would return shortly. The lawmen were leaving when Billy rode up. Conde said he had a warrant to serve and Billy agreed to surrender but wanted to change clothing first. As the pair entered the house, Tom pointed a Winchester at the lawmen.

"You want to arrest Bill, do you? Well you can't do it. I am the one responsible for this business, but you will never take me alive," declared Tom. Eck held the lawmen at gunpoint till Tom and Billy galloped away.

Tom and Billy abandoned their horses about eight miles north of Baker at the Jenkins place. The lawmen found the horses the next evening and suspected that the fugitives had returned to Billy's place. The sheriff and company surrounded the house and watched it all night. Some said they saw men inside. In the morning Sheriff Conde tried to convince Lettie to leave. He did not want to endanger her life if the posse had to open fire with a terrible fusillade. She steadfastly refused. Finally District Attorney Hyde entered the house and talked to Lettie. He became convinced that Tom and Billy were hiding in the house. The officials were considering their options when two volunteers offered to search the house for $5 each. They found nothing and an embarrassed posse returned to Baker on a slow freight train. Tom and Billy may well have been there hiding in a hole dug under the barn. Previously they had cleverly laid a wooden floor covering it. They had often hidden stolen items there. It would have been difficult for them to flee at that time because the rivers were flooding due to recent rains.

Deputy Kennison and detective Farley arrested George at McEwan without incident. They jailed him in Baker overnight. Nellie rode fifty miles to comfort her husband. The next day George was taken to Pendleton and by train to Kittitas County Jail in Ellensburg. He gave a statement while in Pendleton.

"My arrest took me completely by surprise. I am entirely innocent of any complicity in the crime charged. Last September, at the time it is alleged the bank robbery occurred, I believe I was at Cracker Creek; at any rate I can prove an alibi conclusively. I have not been to Washington for nearly four years. During my residence in Baker County I have been in and about Baker City all the time with the exception of a part of the past winter when I went to Utah with Mr. Dalton to negotiate the sale of stock in the Shelton Mine, returning to Baker City about three weeks ago.

"Of my brother Tom, who is the eldest of the family and aged about forty-five years, I have known but little for upwards of fifteen years and have not seen him for two years. I did not know of his presence in the locality of Baker. I have been in the belief that he was in Arizona and engaged in the stock business. The arrest of both of my brothers is as mystifying to me as my own arrest. I do not apprehend any difficulty in securing my acquittal."

Since George had lived near Baker, he had followed mining and sporting—mostly the latter. He was rather stout in build, with "features indicating strength in character and his appearance impresses one favorably," so quoted the *East Oregonian* newspaper.

The local citizens became convinced of the group's guilt after remembering Fred walked with a limp from a gunshot wound received the previous fall. Also Eck had owed his attorney John M. Guerin $500 for two years and paid it shortly after the Roslyn robbery. This was too much to be coincidental since Billy had been close to bankruptcy for some time. All three McCartys were whispered to be "dead-hard game" (slang at the time for desperate men who would do anything for fast, easy money, including murder).

Ellensburg City Marshall McGrath and three deputies went to the cafe in Ephrata, Washington, to arrest Matt. The restaurant had log walls, a canvas roof and rough-hewn tables. Entering, the lawmen asked for a meal and sat down. Matt said he must get water from the spring and left. The lawmen took positions just inside the door and jumped Matt when he entered. Matt was big and strong and resisted violently and shouted for Rosa to get his shotgun. She refused and eventually Matt was subdued and handcuffed.

He was jailed in Ellensburg on May 5. Matt and George stood a preliminary hearing on the seventeenth and bail was set at $10,000 each. The trial date was set for May 22.

Billy wrote a letter to the *Baker City Democrat* from Pocatello, Idaho, and it was reprinted in the *East Oregonian* on April 28, 1893.

> Editors Democrat: As I left your part of the country very suddenly and mysteriously I deem it proper to let my friends in Baker County hear from me, provided you will be so kind as to give space to this letter in the columns of your valuable paper. I want all of my friends to know that neither my brother or I had anything to do with the Roslyn robbery or any other robbery. We have always made our money honestly and if any man wants to look up our pedigree he can easily do so in Colorado, Montana, Nevada or Utah, as we have lived in all those places and can get references from either of the places mentioned.
>
> My reasons for leaving Baker county as I did are as follows: I sold a certain horse to my brother Tom while in the Big Bend country (Ephrata, Washington 7U ranch), and he says the ani-

mal was stolen from him and was used by one of the Roslyn bank robbers. He advised me to pull out until the thing was cleared up; I knew well enough that if I went to the law it would take all I had to prove my innocence I have had something to do with the law in Oregon and Washington and don't want any more of it, and rather take the last cent from my wife and children and see them suffer, I determine to face the strong arm of the law and bid them do their worst. However I assure you that I will vindicate myself in due time.

Tom and I have had a very pleasant trip thus far. We have met with plenty of friends everywhere we have been, who offer us every assistance within their power.

I hope to see you all in the near future. If I had any way of sending you a mess of speckled beauties that abound in the pure mountain streams of these parts I would be pleased to do so. I am badly disfigured but still in the ring. Promising to write you again at some future time, I remain, yours, as ever. W. A. McCarty.

Early in May, Rosa and her daughter took the train to Salt Lake City. They stayed overnight in Pendleton at the Golden Rule Hotel. A reporter stayed overnight in Pendleton at the Golden and interviewed the pretty eighteen-year-old mother. She completely denied all accusations her sister had made. She said Brooks and her sister were not engaged. Her husbands real name was Ray Willard Lewis and he was legitimately engaged in the butcher business. The relationship between her husband and sister was cordial except for one spat. She denied her sister was jailed but was a witness.

Rosa rejoined her family, had a change of heart and wrote the following letter to attorney Snively.

I am the living witness that George McCarty, Bill McCarty, Ras Lewis alias Ras Christiansen, Tom McCarty alias Williams, Fred McCarty and Nellie McCarty are the individuals interested in the above robbery. This, your honor, judge and gentlemen of the jury, I swear by the powers of all heaven and the right of our government, as an honest citizen, the wife of Ras Lewis, alias Christiansen. Now as for dates, as near as I can remember, about the 10th of September, they just met to our house planning the robbery, they left about the 12th. In about two weeks Ras Lewis went to them and returned either the 1st or 2nd of October. That was the last I saw of them until November 12, 1892, when Billy, Tom and Fred McCarty came to plan another and would have gone but for my interference. I swear to what my sister, Sarah Jane Morgan, has said, that is the truth only, so help me God. Rosa Willard is my marriage name, Christiansen in Oregon, Lewis in Washington. Am also witness for five other robberies, train, bank and store.

About 3 P.M. on Sunday, May 21, Matt and George were exercising in the jail corridor. They picked up a double-pointed crowbar from its hiding place and quickly broke a man-sized hole in the outer jail wall. Crawling through, they ran across the jail yard and scaled the fence. At the end of the alley they reached under some loose boards in the sidewalk and grabbed two Colt revolvers. Ed Grady and Mose Bowman were returning from a morning bird hunt and saw the pair running up Sixth Street. Firing shotguns, they wounded both with birdshot. George returned fire, slightly wounding young Billy Hayes in his arm. They ran into J. C. Clymer's house and apologized to Mrs. Clymer and her young son for bothering them. Quickly the house was surrounded by armed and irate citizens.

City Marshall McGrath went to the door and Matt invited him in. Matt said he didn't want to hurt anyone and would willingly return to jail if the marshall would disperse the crowd. He demanded to see Joe Brooks "to settle some business." McGrath agreed to handle the crowd but Brooks was not in town. George and Matt were allowed to keep their revolvers while walking back to the jail. Several lawmen escorted the pair to the jail where they surrendered the revolvers. Many citizens armed themselves and loitered by the jail all night. Witnesses said a man leading two saddled horses had approached the Clymer house during the escape but disappeared when the crowd surrounded it.

The jail was searched, and sewn into George's vest were eighteen hacksaw blades with two wooden frames. A brace with several bits was found. Under the loose boards in the sidewalk a deputy removed a Winchester rifle. The trial started the next morning.

Cashier Abernathy was the first witness. He identified Matt as his assailant. Dr. Lyons and other witnesses verified that. Sarah Jane Morgan testified that while she was helping Matt and Rosa she learned about the robbery. Matt had left in mid-September saying he was going to rob a bank with the McCartys. When he returned, Sarah helped him count his share—about $1,100. He returned on a gray horse that had been shot in its jaw. The horse was later shot and skinned by Hank Vaughn. A belt that Matt had custom made in Coulee City was introduced; it had pouches for money and cartridges.

Ole Hansen told of meeting the robbers and guiding them to the Columbia River by lantern light. He had spoken to Matt in Danish before Matt struck him. Joe Brooks testified and Matt swore to kill him.

The defense called Cashier Abernathy and made a strong point that previously he had identified Cal Hale as his assailant. Abernathy said he might have been mistaken. The defense also called other witnesses that still maintained that Cal Hale was a robber. This caused some doubt and the jury deadlocked—eight for guilty and four not guilty. Matt was held for another trial in September.

George's trial was almost a carbon copy of Matt's. J. M. McDonald testified that George was one of the horse holders. Other witnesses said he was involved and some placed him in the Roslyn area in September. George and Nellie claimed they were prospecting on Swauk or Tarpestan Creeks in September. The jury deadlocked, seven guilty and five not. George was held for a new trial in September.

Injustice prevailed because of human error. Ben Snipes was a millionaire in 1892. In seeking revenge he spent more than $8,000 retaining Thiel Detective Agency and attorneys to assist the prosecution. Kittitas County spent over $3,000 trying Hale, Kinsey and Zachery. The cases against Matt and George cost about $1,200. The county operating capital was on deposit in Snipes' bank. On June 9 the bank closed its doors forever having failed because of the Panic of '93 and Snipes' error. The depositors, including the county, received ten cents for each dollar on deposit. Thus, there was no money available to retry Matt and George. The prosecution reluctantly moved to dismiss charges on September 6. Both were immediately rearrested and charged with escape and assault. The charges were dismissed just as quickly for the same reason.

Several years later Sullivan was walking on a street in Tacoma. A man confronted him and called him a name that usually caused a fight. Sullivan did not respond, so the man slapped him. Sullivan collapsed and died a few minutes later. Cal Hale never fully recovered from his ordeal. He had sold all of his valuables and gave a $75 promissory note to pay his attorney. The note was never paid. Later he was judged insane and committed to an asylum where he stayed for eight years and then was released.

Frank A. Abernathy also suffered from mental illness and became a fellow inmate of Hale. He never recovered and died in the asylum. Ben Snipes suffered further financial reversals till he died penniless in 1906.

Returning briefly to April of 1893, detective Farley had an arrest warrant for Tom. He was charged with the March 29, 1889, robbery of the First National Bank in Denver. In that case a man entered that bank just after lunch and requested an interview with President Moffat. Upon entering Moffat's office he said that a bank robbery was planned and was soon to be effected. Then he displayed a small bottle of liquid he claimed was nitroglycerin. He then drew his revolver and instructed Moffat to write a counter check for $21,000 and cash it. With no choice, Moffat complied. The teller gave him $20,000 in currency and $1,000 in gold. One bill was a $10,000 bank note. The robber departed quickly with the money. He was soon lost in street traffic.

A very detailed description was given to police and it resembled Tom but it wasn't. Several suspects were sought and arrested but none went to trial. The bottle's contents were determined to be castor oil. This was not Tom's method of operation. He denied it in his autobiography.

Returning to November of 1892, when Sullivan was arresting the wrong men a train was robbed in Washington. Just west of the crest of the Cascade Mountains in Stampede Pass is Hot Springs, a settlement comprising a railroad station and a few buildings near the tracks of the Northern Pacific. The westbound train stopped there at 9:30 P.M. on November 24. Three men boarded and entered the passenger coach announcing a robbery by firing a shot into the ceiling. The frightened passengers readily surrendered their money and valuables. Then one of the bandits pulled the bell wire properly and the train stopped just west of Maywood. The robbers were about $1,200 richer as they fled into the cold, snowy darkness. Since they had all worn masks, only poor descriptions were obtained by responding deputies. The leader swore constantly. One had a thirty-year-old cap and ball revolver.

The Northern Pacific offered a $500 reward. Sheriff Woolery and deputies searched for clues by attending a ball at the hotel. They played cards and made frequent trips to a saloon. None followed the outlaws' tracks because fresh snow quickly covered them.

Tom said in his autobiography that they robbed a Northern Pacific train during this time period. He also said they had a new partner and traveled around Washington briefly before returning to Billy's ranch.

Early in the fall of 1893, Tom, Billy and Fred went to Robbers Roost to plan another job. Matt went to work near Vernal. George and Nellie concentrated on mining near Baker.

Delta, Colorado, had been founded in 1882 on the Gunnison River. By 1893, it boasted of a population of 1,500. Local farmers and ranchers filled the Farmers and Merchants Bank with money. Tom and Billy rode into Delta late in the afternoon of September 6. They registered at the Central Hotel as brothers James G. and Clarence Bradley. After a fine supper they each enjoyed a cigar and drinks. The next morning they breakfasted at the hotel dining room. Fred had stayed with the relay horses at their camp and rode into town in the late forenoon. They strolled casually around town and Tom bought a bottle of whiskey. He sipped from it occasionally.

About 10 A.M. the trio rode their horses into the alley behind the bank. Tom, as usual, held the horses while Billy and Fred entered. Andrew Blachly was typing and H. H. Wolbert was busy bookkeeping. Fred jumped over the low counter and drew his revolver. Billy covered the clerk and demanded all the money. Both men refused, Fred cursed and Wolbert reached for a hidden revolver. Blachly yelled and Fred shot and killed him. Firing another shot into the floor then, grabbing money from the cash drawers, Fred stuffed the money in a canvas sack. Billy and Fred pushed Wolbert out the back door and saw that Tom was holding attorney W. R. Robertson at gunpoint. The pair mounted and all three galloped south down the alley leaving Wolbert and Robertson staring at them in amazement. Some of the money fell out of the sack to scatter in the alley dust.

Hardware clerk W. R. Simpson heard the gunfire and picked up his Sharps .45-70 and some cartridges and ran into the street. The three bandits were bent low over their horses and racing away. Simpson fired at Billy, about 240 feet distance. The bullet struck him in the back of his head killing him instantly. Simpson reloaded as Fred stopped and turned to see his father fall. Simpson fired again killing Fred with another head shot at 385 feet, the bullet then lodged in the neck of Fred's horse severing its jugular vein. It took a few steps and died. Simpson's third bullet missed but a fourth nicked the leg of Tom's horse. Simpson became a living legend for his excellent marksmanship.

Almost $1,000 had been taken but $700 was recovered from Billy and $300 found scattered in the alley. Someone cut the tail from Fred's horse and nailed it to a wall in the blacksmith shop. It remained there till the building was demolished years later. Andrew Blachly left a widow and seven children.

The sheriff formed a posse but couldn't catch Tom. Later they took Billy's horse north out of town and removed its tack and freed it. It led them straight to the outlaws' camp where the relay horses had been hidden. No clues were found to identify the dead men. Later a citizen who knew the McCartys identified Billy and Fred.

Above: Fred McCarty, son of Bill McCarty, murderer of A.T. Blachly, Delta bank robbery, 1893.
Photo: Colorado Historical Society

Right: Bill McCarty, bank robber, Delta, 1893.
Photo: Colorado Historical Society

Tom rode a lot of miles looking over his shoulder. He slept lightly and well hidden. He stayed hidden for a long while.

Northeast of Pendleton in 1893 was the town of Milton. (The name was changed in 1951 to Milton-Freewater.) In early November three men familiarized themselves with the area. In Pendleton they sold two horses at Beales Feedyard. They ate at Killian's place in Vancycle. They bought wirecutters and cut fences while laying false trails. Between Athena and Weston they ate at the Richardson place.

Monday, November 13, 1893, was foggy around Milton. Just at 3 P.M. the three rode into town and dismounted at the Bank of Milton. One held the horses and the two bigger men entered. Drawing revolvers they demanded money from president A. Hopson, cashier N. A. Davis and Hopson's son, an assistant cashier. The elder Hopson reached for a hidden revolver and both gunmen fired wounding Hopson. Cashier Davis was so close to one revolver that he suffered powder burns on his face. Young Hopson quickly handed over $994.25 mostly in gold coins. The bandits rushed out and all three galloped away. They rode toward Basket Mountain. Within ten minutes Deputy Sheriff Richey started in pursuit with a four-man posse. The bandits had not worn masks in the bank, but they masked themselves as they rode away. Two witnesses said they recognized a McCarty brother from North Powder. Two robbers were about thirty and one about twenty or so. Their horses were black, bay and iron gray.

The bank soon offered a reward of $300 plus half of any recovered money. Sheriff Furnish offered $200 dead or alive. Hopson's wound was superficial and he was back on the job the next day.

Fog limited visibility to less than 200 yards and early darkness combined to make pursuit useless. Early Tuesday several posses rode out to find false trails and cut barb wire. Wednesday Chris Breding went to his vacant farm about nine miles from Pendleton. In the barn he found the bandits' horses exhausted and thirsty. Their tack had been neatly put away. He cared for the animals and on Friday went to Pendleton and learned of the robbery.

He notified the sheriff who showed the horses to witnesses who declared they were the bandits' mounts.

On Thursday evening two Pendleton residents returning from a visit saw three men walking along railroad tracks. They fit the bandits' description. It wasn't long before the westbound train stopped and they weren't seen again. The posses were called in and the robbery became history.

It was not known to many, but a McCarty brother had lived the life of retirement at Martha Vaughn's home for some time. He had a gray mare that he broke and trained. Witnesses who saw the horse identified it as the one ridden in the robbery. For a short time it was speculated that Hugh Robey, Martha's eldest son was the young bandit. Then it was discovered that he had been a posse member. George and Matt bore a remarkable resemblance to the descriptions.

In 1932, Rufus Woods, editor of Washington's *The Wenatchee Daily World*, interviewed Tom Cook, an Ephrata merchant. Cook said he knew Ras Lewis and heard the shooting when Matt made Rosa do the six-gun dance. He also said that Joe Brook's body was found on a sandbar in the Snake River a few days before the Milton robbery. Death records were not required before 1907 so this cannot be verified.

The year 1894 saw the death of Doctor Alexander G. McCarty on November 26, in Myrtle Creek, Oregon, at the age of 73. After the death of her husband, Mary Ann Palmer McCarty resided with her youngest daughter till she died at the age of 83 on October 9, 1913. She was buried next to her husband in Myrtle Creek.

The Washauer Hotel in Baker offered the finest accommodations between Salt Lake City and Portland. The casino catered to the gambling public. On December 2, 1894, at 2:30 A.M., six masked and heavily armed men entered the casino demanding money and valuables. The till produced $40, the crap table $370 and the faro table $660. A patron sneaked out and ran up Front Street shouting holdup. Policeman Witt ran to the hotel and turned in a fire alarm. The gunmen disappeared before the firemen arrived.

In due course several men were arrested. J. D. Hart had paid a bill and displayed a lot of cash just after the robbery. He said he borrowed the money from Albert Vaughn, Hank and Lois' son. Hart had a credible alibi as he was sipping beer at the Brunswick Beer Hall during the robbery. Eventually all were released for lack of evidence. A casino robbery was mentioned in Matt Warner's book and Tom McCarty's autobiography. This undoubtedly was it.

In the late fall of 1895, Robert Swift found rich ore in Dry Fork Canyon twenty miles north of Vernal, Utah. Very close by David Milton also found a promising outcrop of ore. As winter closed in at the high elevation Swift and Milton left and planned to return in the spring to do development work. Swift's big mouth was his worst enemy because he told E. B. Coleman, and soon Ike and Dick Staunton knew of the find. Greed guided their actions as the snow began to melt. In May of '96 Dave Milton and Bob Swift were camped at the snow line. Coleman visited their camps and demanded a share of the mine. Coleman and Swift had previously been partners in other properties. The Staunton brothers camped with Milton. Coleman negotiated a deal, for $500 the Stauntons and Milton would not follow Coleman for ten days. Coleman went to Vernal and borrowed $500 and hired Matt and William Wall to jump the claims. Matt paid his bar tab and gave his mother-in-law $24 to hold for him. The trio arrived at the campsites at dawn and made their final plans. The Stauntons and Milton were still in their tents. Warner and Wall rode in fast and, dismounting, opened fire. Dick Staunton and Milton were fatally wounded. Ike was also wounded but eventually recovered. It was over in ten seconds. The participants then recognized one another as friends. Warner and Wall made the wounded comfortable and Bob Swift went to Vernal for a wagon. They carried the wounded to Vernal arriving about midnight.

Matt Warner, William Wall and E. B. Coleman were arrested and charged with murder. The trial was held in Ogden and start-

41

Washauer Hotel In Baker, Oregon, whose casino was robbed December 2, 1894. In the 1990s it was restored to its original splendor and is the Giesler Grand now.

Photo: Oregon Trail Regional Museum

Bourne Bar, formerly Cracker City. George worked here placering gold from 1884 to 1891. When the brothers got together they probably drank here. The bar is now in the Eastern Oregon Museum in Haines, Oregon.

Photo: Eastern Oregon Museum

Above: Cell block in Utah State Prison, circa 1909.

Photo: Utah State Historical Society

Right: Interior of cell in Utah State Prison, circa 1909.

Photo: Utah State Historical Society

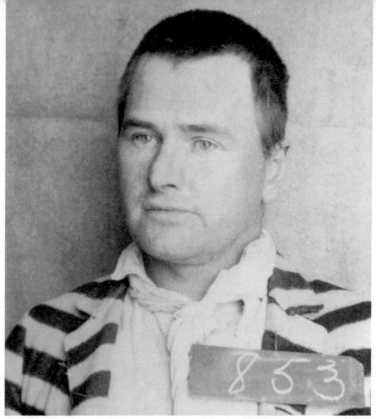

Erastus Christiansen, alias Matt Warner, when he entered Utah State Prison in
September, 1896.
Photo: Utah State Archives

Lewis McCarty who was the
eldest son of Tom and Teenie.
Photo: Jim Beckstead

ed in September. The testimony was contradictory on every point. After three days Coleman was declared innocent and freed. The jury finally agreed that it was a free for all gunfight. Warner and Wall were found guilty of manslaughter. Before sentencing Judge Powers read a number of letters written to Matt from Rosa. They were extremely affectionate in character and went far to remove the impression from the mind of the court that Matt abused his wife. That conflicted with Rosa's mother's testimony. She told that Matt had given her $24 to hold for him and she dare not give it to Rosa for the necessities of life. She feared he would retaliate if she did. The sheriff and one deputy took the prisoners to Utah State Prison on the 2:10 Union Pacific. Both served three years and four months. With good behavior, that was the standard time for a five-year sentence.

Lois McCarty Vaughn Hunsaker died in 1896 while working in her garden. Her nine-year-old son was with her but the rest of the family was away. The boy covered his mother's body with rocks to protect it from destruction by coyotes or buzzards. She was given a proper funeral and internment.

That same year Lewis McCarty and Henry Malmgren were found guilty of rustling in Manti, Utah. Lewis was Tom's son who had been raised by his maternal grandparents in Levan. The pair had stolen about thirty head and when arrested Grandpa posted $1,000 bail. The jury in the first trial deadlocked. Sentencing was scheduled for 11 A.M. the next morning. Neils Jorgensen was a kindhearted jailer and the rustlers took advantage of it. After supper they asked to step outside for a last breath of free air. Jorgensen granted the request and escorted them downstairs to the sidewalk. Instantly they ran in opposite directions and, stealing horses, made a clean getaway. Jorgensen ran to the livery stable and found both of their horses saddled. No attempt was made to apprehend them. Lewis was listed in the 1900 census as a bartender living in Price, county seat of adjoining Carbon County.

About nine miles north of Price up a steep-sided narrow canyon was the coal mining town of Castle Gate. The Pleasant

Above and below foreground: Headquarters of the Pleasant Valley Coal Company which Tom McCarty and Butch Cassidy robbed in April of 1897. Butch Cassidy waited at the foot of the outside stairs to rob E. L. Carpenter who carried most of the money. Tom McCarty held the horses closeby.

Photo: Western Mining & Railroad Museum, Helper, Utah

Valley Coal Company regularly paid its miners in gold coin. Tom McCarty and Butch Cassidy reunited and arrived in Castle Gate in mid-April of 1897. Ordinary horsemen were a rarity in mining towns. However, horse races were common and well attended. Tom and Butch represented themselves as race horse trainers. Butch rode a fine fast horse with a suringle, which is a wide belt around the horse's midsection with stirrups. Both met the daily train on horseback and calmed their mounts when the train made noise or let off steam. Tom spent a lot of time in Caffeys Saloon.

The Rio Grande and Western Railroad passenger train number three from Salt Lake City arrived in Castle Gate at noon on April 21, 1897. It was payday for the miners. Paymaster E. L. Carpenter and his assistant T. W. Lewis picked up two sacks of silver coins containing $1,000 and $960 and a third sack containing $7,000 in gold from the express car. They also picked up a satchel of checks and walked across the tracks to the company office about fifty yards away.

Butch Cassidy was sitting on a box at the foot of the outside stairs leading to the second-floor paymaster office. When Carpenter and Lewis reached the stairs Butch drew his revolver and commanded, "Drop them sacks and hold up your hands." Lewis dropped his sacks and bolted into a store. Carpenter dropped the sack and satchel. Butch picked them up handing them to Tom who tied them to his saddle but in doing so dropped the reins of Butch's horse. The horse became frightened by the rapid movements and the train noise and escaping steam. Butch was an excellent horseman and caught and mounted the horse quickly and the pair galloped away. A clerk in the upstairs office fired a rifle shot at the pair, but Tom returned three shots discouraging the clerk. They stopped behind the power house where Butch removed the suringle and saddled his horse with a proper saddle hidden there the previous evening. Tom found nothing valuable in the satchel and determined the heavy bag of silver would slow them down so he discarded both. Then they rode south and cut telegraph wires. A well-known Scotsman at Castle Gate became so excited that he mounted a horse and followed the bandits for three miles. He was unarmed but shouted, "Bring that money back!" He was ignored.

Carpenter was taken by surprise but reacted quickly by rushing to the train cab and taking control. The cars were cut loose and the throttle opened. The whistle was tied down and the train sped down the canyon to Price. It arrived there before the outlaws did. Telegraphers were busy spreading the news to local lawmen. Posses left Castle Gate, Huntington and Price. L. S. Dickerson in Salt Lake City formed a posse and departed by train for Green River. He was hoping to intercept the robbers before they reached Robbers Roost, possibly in San Rafael Canyon.

Butch and Tom had circled Price and rode south through Cleveland. Many people saw them cut a fence in Cleveland and ride toward Peters Spring ten miles away. They arrived there about 6 P.M. and Anton Neilsen was waiting with the relay horses. By 7 P.M. they had Cedar Mountain behind them and were moving down San Rafael River Canyon. After passing Sulphur Springs they went up Black Dragon Wash and then north to Tidwells Draw. By Friday they were in the Dirty Devil River area of Robbers Roost.

The third partner was Joe Walker who had stolen three fine horses from the Whitmore Ranch in March. He was married to a sister of the Whitmore brothers who despised him.

Butch and Tom had boarded a horse with Jens Neilsen all winter. Neilsen later told that the bandits were respectful and paid well. His young son Anton had delivered the relay horses to Peters Spring. He was shown a drawing of Butch and he declared it vaguely resembled him. Butch had used the alias Fowler and Tom was Tom Gillies. Gillies was the maiden name of Butch's mother. County attorney W. F. Warf identified Gillies as Lewis McCarty, with whom he was acquainted. Witnesses described the bandits as one about thirty and one middle aged. Elzy Lay, alias William McGinnis, was two years younger than Butch but was credited with this robbery.

Tom and Butch had been seen in Green River accompanied by two women. They had bought a wagon load of supplies and all the ammunition in town. Then they disappeared.

In late April of 1898, Joe Walker and three lesser known rustlers stole several fine horses from the Whitmores. Then they stole twenty-five head of cattle from two drovers whom they brutally assaulted. Previously Governor Heber Wells had offered a $500 reward for Joe Walker for rustling and wounding Sheriff Ebenezer Tuttle. Sheriff Allred of Carbon County, Sheriff Tuttle of Emery County, Joe Bush and George C. Whitmore and others formed a posse that resolved to capture Joe Walker.

They were on the trail for about ten days finally reaching the North Fork of Florence Creek. Then the outlaw camp was located and before dawn it was surrounded. The sheriff shouted for their surrender. Thompson and Shultz quickly raised their hands. Walker and John Herron opened fire but were killed immediately. The posse thought Herron was Butch Cassidy and mentally spent the reward money during the long, difficult ride back. Herron was buried as Cassidy but later dug up and identified. Shultz and Thompson were released for lack of evidence.

In the fall of 1895, George and three partners found the Flagstaff Mine near Baker. In March of 1896 it was sold to a large French mining company for $51,000. Actually, they weren't partners, but they owned twenty-one adjacent mining claims. The buyers wanted all the claims in order to operate the mines economically. By August, 200 men were employed to recover gold. The 1900 census records George and Nellie living on interest dividends. The Vaughn brothers once salted a mine and sold it. Their stepfather Joe Hunsaker made them return the money. Then good fortune smiled on the Vaughns and Hunsakers. They found the Iron Dyke Mine and sold it for $43,000 shaking hands on the deal. The very next day they were offered substantially more for it but declined the offer. Production records disclose that from 1910–34, 34,000 ounces of gold, 265,000 ounces of silver and 14,000,000 pounds of copper were mined.

Sheriff John H. Ward of Unita County, Wyoming, wrote Utah Governor Wells about Matt Warner. He suggested that Governor Wells encourage the district attorney of Telluride, Colorado, to prosecute Warner for bank robbery stating, "knowing as you do that Warner has not and will not reform." The Governor responded saying he was in complete agreement noting that he was fully convinced that Warner was resolved to being a lifelong outlaw and a tough. He wrote Governor Adams of Colorado advising him of their opinions. Colorado did not prosecute.

Tom's youngest son, Leonard, enlisted in Battery B of the Utah Light Artillery on May 5, 1898. He sailed on the SS *China* to the Philippine Islands. His battery participated in several artillery duels during the next year. He liked the Filipinos and learned much of their language. He was discharged in San Francisco, August 16, 1899. He returned to Utah with the battalion to a big homecoming celebration.

After his uncle Matt was released from prison, they became partners in supplying horses to the British Army for use during the Boer War. They filled two contracts then he became a bartender in Green River, a job he hated. He married Della McIntire and eventually had three boys.

Matt Warner settled in Price and worked at various jobs. Rosa and his children had died while he was in prison. He remarried and had a small family. He operated the Mint Saloon and was a Justice of the Peace in East Carbon for one term. He was night marshall in Price for two terms and ran for sheriff in 1912. He ran as W. E. Christiansen, but was known as Matt Warner and came in fourth. During prohibition he was a bootlegger. He died in December of 1938.

George and Nellie lived on the Idaho side of the Snake River across from Homestead, Oregon. George built a house on a steep hillside near a year-round spring. A pine tree grew through the porch roof and the rear wall almost touched the hillside. George

McCarty Bridge Road. The brothers built a bridge over the Powder River about one hundred yards from Interstate 84-30, the old Oregon Trail, in the 1880s. It has been replaced twice.   *Photo: Norman Davis*

George and Nellie McCarty rest for all eternity in Pine Haven Cemetary in Halfway, Oregon.   *Photo: Norman Davis*

located the Paymaster nearby. It had a six-foot vein of ore that produced for years. He grew fruit, especially strawberries—large, red, sweet ones. He sold them in Homestead for a dollar a bucket. The children of Homestead would visit George and Nellie when the berries were ripe and never went home disappointed. George had a cat and Nellie had a cat. They also shared the affection and companionship of the dog and pet rooster. Nellie would buy a can of red salmon for her cat and George would buy a can of pink salmon for his cat. Their cats were very personal.

They had an Edison Cylinder Phonograph. In the evenings sitting by a kerosene lamp, they would enjoy the voice of Enrico Caruso in that remote deepest canyon in North America.

In the evening of January 31, 1937, George returned from working and found Nellie had died while preparing supper. The Snake River was full of floating ice so her body was placed in a cable car and pulled over to the Oregon side. She was buried in Pine Haven Cemetery in Halfway, Oregon.

George lived alone till one night in 1946. Someone piled brush against the house and set it afire. George ran out in his long underwear and someone shot at him but missed. He ran to the river and rowed his boat across to Homestead. That was the third attempt to burn him out. He never returned and lived with friends in Halfway till he died October 28, 1948. He rests beside Nellie for all eternity. Without a doubt he was the last horse and revolver bandit.

During April and May of 1899 Butch Cassidy was living near Browns Peak some fifty miles northeast of Vernal, Utah. His companions were Elzy Lay and Tom McCarty. Lay was married in 1896 to Maude Davis; her father lived in Vernal. Butch kept company with a prominent, well-respected lady. Sheriff Allred was informed of their whereabouts and that they were planning a train robbery. Allred thought the plan was to rob the Rio Grande Western between Price and Thompsons. However plans had to be altered because prospectors were numerous in the area because of a recent copper strike. Convinced the information was reliable Allred notified Doc Shores of the Rio Grande Western.

Three men were staying briefly in Kemmerer, Wyoming. They bought a team and wagon, a complete camping outfit, a Winchester rifle, horses and in particular a pinto from William Fenn. On April fifteenth they drove east. They met Butch, Tom and Elzy Lay near Wilcox, Wyoming, about forty-four miles west of Laramie.

Shortly after 2 A.M. on June 2, 1899, the Union Pacific *Westbound Transcontinental Fast Mail* was moving on an upgrade at fifty miles per hour. W. T. (Grindstone) Jones, the engineer, saw a red and white signal by the tracks. That was the emergency stop signal so the brakes were applied and the train stopped at 2:18 A.M. Four masked bandits entered the cab and took command. Other bandits uncoupled the few passenger cars and Grindstone was ordered to pull ahead. He responded too slowly and a bandit struck his head with his revolver barrel. The wound bled profusely.

The bandit leader commanded, "Hold there, we don't want any killing about this." There was no more violence. The train crew said there was a second section and it was loaded with army troops and it was close behind. This was a ruse as there were no soldiers, but there was a second section. The train was stopped on the far side of a bridge and the bandits exploded dynamite, which spread the rails. That would stop the second section. Then the train moved to the bandits' camp.

There the leader went to the mail car and ordered the clerks W. G. Bruce and L. L. Detrick out. Bruce told him to go to hell

52

and turned out the lights. The bandits shot into the car from all angles then the leader exploded dynamite on the door sill. The clerks came out but the mail was not disturbed. Moving to the express car, Ernest Woodcock refused to leave the car when ordered. The bandits shot into the car and exploded dynamite on the door sill. Woodcock was stunned and was helped out and relieved of a shotgun and a revolver. All concerned moved about fifty yards from the car and twenty sticks of dynamite were exploded on top of the safe. The express car was ruined and the safe split wide open. The contents were carried off by five bandits making two trips each. Just before 4 A.M. the bandits walked off into the darkness. It was another two hours before the train could move again.

The Union Pacific officials said only a few hundred dollars were taken. Clerks and others speculated that probably $36,000 in cash and about $6–10,000 in diamonds was a more realistic figure. Immediately rewards of $1,000 each were offered and quickly raised to $3,000.

The bandit leader was described as fifty years old, 5'7" to 5'8", thin round nose, large eyes with small eyeballs, 150 to 160 pounds. He had a nasal twang or high-pitched voice.

Tom McCarty was a few months short of his forty-ninth birthday. He was 5'7 1/8", and weight unknown at that time. He weighed 127 pounds in 1913. A profile photo shows a rounded nose. His eyes match the description in a 1913 photo.

Number two had a dark complexion, black woolly hair, was 5'9" or 10", about 170 pounds. This could have been either Elzy Lay or Harry "Sundance Kid" Longabaugh. Number three was 5'8" or 9", black hair, 160 or 170 pounds. This was probably Flat Nose George Curry. Number four was quite small, about 5'6", dark complexion about 160 pounds. Possibly this was Harvey Logan, alias Kid Curry. The fifth man weighed about 150 pounds and had a Texas accent. This was probably Bill Carver. The sixth man was 5'8" or 9", 150 pounds, stubby sandy beard—probably Butch Cassidy.

Later a modified description of one man was published. He was thirty-one or thirty-two years old, 5'8" or 9", 185 pounds, complexion and hair light, blue eyes and a peculiar nose—flattened at bridge and heavy at point. He had a full red face, was slightly stooping, slightly bow legged and had a bald forehead. This had to be Flat Nose George Curry. This is a good description considering that it was dark and the bandits wore masks.

Several posses were sent out by late morning. One found the trail and followed it north for miles. Recent rains made the ground ideal for tracking. So the bandits rode into buffalo grass and split up, three and three. Three rode north and Butch, Tom and Elzy rode south through Horsethief Canyon. The posse lost the trail.

On June 4, a posse thirty miles north of Casper saw the bandits. The bandits were riding tired horses and had rested them as they ate lunch near Teapot Creek. Undoubtedly they had seen their pursuers approach and shot, killing some horses. The posse took cover and returned two shots but couldn't locate the bandits. The bandits were using new smokeless gun powder. The bandits slipped away but left behind Woodcock's shotgun, which was marked Pacific Express Co. On June 5, ten miles further into the rough and wild country a second engagement was fought. The bandits with exhausted horses had hid in rocks and fired as the posse approached. Sheriff Hazen was mortally wounded and taken by wagon and train to his home in Douglas where he died.

Hazen was only forty-four years old and left a widow and two small boys. The Union Pacific Railroad contributed $2,400 and the governor started a fund to pay off a $300 mortgage on his home. The death caused the public to concentrate their efforts to capture the bandits and lynching was openly discussed. Major C. H. Parmalee ordered a detail of state militia to assist Marshall Hadsell. Regular U.S. Army troops were ordered into the chase. On June 11, decisions were made to rid the country once and for all of the Hole in the Wall Gang.

Heads of railroads, corporations and cattle companies called for 200 men to volunteer in the manhunt. Detectives were to be assisted by old-time frontiersmen, Native American fighters, cowboys, trackers and Native police. They would be equipped and fed by the cattle, railroad and business men. Every man was to be fearless and a dead shot with a strong resolve to succeed. This sounded good in the newspapers, but little was accomplished as time passed. Eventually the search on horseback ended and the detectives asked questions and traced the money. Tired horses were found by posses and stabled in Laramie. Later they were identified by witnesses from Kemmerer.

The lady in Vernal confirmed that Butch was involved in the robbery. He and his partners spent a week in a bordello then rode east in late May. A well-known cattleman of Price was firm in his belief that Cassidy, Lay and old Tom McCarty were the three unidentified bandits.

Tom and Butch probably went to their previous winter quarters. That was in Robbers Roost high on a mesa between Horseshoe Canyon and Dennis Canyon. They had a 12 x 16 ft. tent near a rock fort they had built. There was only one way up there and two ways down. To go down into Dennis Canyon, they had to jump their horses ten feet. The other way was near the head of Horseshoe Canyon and also was difficult to negotiate.

It is possible that the reason Tom McCarty held the horses in previous robberies was because of his high-pitched voice. It was not an ominous, commanding voice, thus might be ignored causing serious problems. At Wilcox he participated as an experienced leader. His orders were followed exactly by all of those present.

Tom must have decided after almost thirty years of banditry to quit. Eventually his good luck would have run out. This was reinforced as each of his contemporaries was caught or killed. Elzy Lay, Bill Carver and others robbed a train near Folsom, New Mexico, about six weeks after the Wilcox robbery. Sam Ketchum and Elzy were wounded by a posse. Ketchum died and Elzy went to prison. Bill Carver was killed by a sheriff near Sonora, Texas. Tom Ketchum was hanged for robbing the same train shortly after his brother Sam did.

Flat Nose George Curry had enough of train robberies and returned to rustling. On the afternoon of April 19, 1900, he was changing brands on cattle owned by the Webster Cattle Company near Castle, Utah. Sheriff Tyler of Grand County ordered him to surrender. Curry opened fire and was killed in a brief gun battle.

Robert E. Lee was dealing cards in Cripple Creek, Colorado, in March of 1900. Seven lawmen surrounded him and he was arrested. He was convicted of mail robbery and sent to Wyoming State Prison on May 31, 1900. He served seven years.

The same day that Lee was arrested Lonnie Logan was killed by a posse in Dodson, Missouri. Harvey Logan participated in the train holdup near Wagner, Montana. He was tracked to Knoxville, Tennessee, and arrested. He escaped after being sentenced to twenty years. Several stories conflict as to his fate, none of which are definite.

Tom eventually started working for wages as a teamster in Salt Lake City for the Utah Construction Company. When laid off, he would work for other construction companies. He even worked for the railroad.

Tom, Charles Watt and Louis Mitchell drew their pay after being laid off from the railroad near Price, Utah. Early in the afternoon of September 27, 1913, they began drinking. Mitchell had rented room six in the Price Hotel and the trio went to the room early in the evening. Mitchell went to sleep. Tom and Charles were still thirsty; however, they had spent all of their money. They stole less than twenty dollars from Mitchell who woke up. They apologized for taking his money and returned to the saloon. Mitchell swore out a warrant and they were arrested and held on $1,000 bail. Tom gave his name as John Lewis to the booking officer. By October 24, District Attorney J. W. Cherry had convinced both to plead guilty to third-degree burglary. He neglected to tell them that Louis Mitchell had left town and his whereabouts were unknown. Thus, without a complaining witness there was no case. Had they demanded a trial they would have been released. Tom then told Judge Christianson his name was John McCarty and received sixty days to three years in prison. The judge recommended a term of eighteen months.

Tom didn't know or care that his family was close by. Lewis was a bartender in Price. Leonard was a bartender in Green River about sixty miles east. Leonards' wife and children had been in Price attending the fair in late September. Matt Warner was living in Price.

Above: This photocopy of an original photograph no longer in existence proves Tom McCarty had a round nose and was the leader of the robbers at Wilcox, Wyoming, June 2, 1899.

Photo: Utah State Archives

Right: Tom McCarty when he entered Utah State Prison in October, 1913.

Photo: Utah State Archives

When Tom applied for a pardon on May 14, 1914, he learned his scheduled release date was set for October 26, 1915. Tom reminded the board that his conduct was exemplary. The board reset his release date for July 19, 1915. There is no evidence that anyone knew that he was the famous outlaw wanted in Arizona, Utah, Colorado, Washington and Oregon. Actually the statute of limitations had long since run out. Witnesses and evidence had disappeared many years previously. So after serving twenty-one months, he was released. He next appeared in Denver, Colorado, in 1918.

Denver was a haven for senior citizens with limited means of support. Its citizens were generous in helping the less fortunate with life's basic necessities. People with sickness and disabilities brought on by years of alcohol abuse were treated. Tuberculars found some relief in its beneficial climate. Tom had broken his right hand and it hadn't healed properly. His left middle finger was misshapen and amputated at the third joint. Tom's final residence was the Saxon Hotel at 1108 22nd Street. He worked occasionally as a laborer. In August of 1926 he became ill and bedridden. He was depressed and told fellow tenants he was going to kill himself.

On the morning of September 7, he wearily rose from his bed and went to the bathroom at the end of the hall. He filled the tub and drowned himself. Mr. Mason saw water running on the hall floor and entered the bathroom to find Tom dead. He laid his body on the floor and eventually coroner George A. Collins arrived. His death was determined as a suicide. He was buried at county expense in Riverside Cemetery, section 80, lot 17, block 12. There is no stone just a concrete marker the size of a coffee can numbered 17.

Tom had broken all family ties decades previously. In choosing September 7, he showed his love and respect for Billy and Fred. They died on that date thirty-three years earlier in a dusty street of Delta, Colorado. He died a penniless nobody in a skid row flophouse as John T. McCarty, not as the famous outlaw Tom McCarty. He must have known no one would know the significance of September 7. No one did for more than seventy years.

Martha Robey lived on the Umatilla Indian Reservation till she died.

In Unitah County, Utah, are the Unita Mountains. Calder Pond was on Pot Creek at the head of Jackson Draw. The name was changed to Matt Warner Reservoir.

Baker City, Oregon, was known as "Queen of the Mines" for several decades after 1870. The Washauer Hotel was the finest hotel between Salt Lake City and Portland, Oregon. A 200-seat dining room served Maine lobsters and Chesapeake Bay Blue Point oysters. Two saloons and a casino offered other pleasures. The name was changed to Geiser Grand. In the 1990s it was refurbished to its original splendor with antiques and custom furniture. Bathrooms have been built in the rooms as it is no longer acceptable for rowdy citizens to shoot revolvers at the cupola as they did in the past.

Though they never made a fortune, the McCarty clan will live on in infamy and legend in the wilds of the American northwest.

STATE OF COLORADO

Certificate of Death

169 8242

PLACE OF DEATH

County D

Town E

or City V

No. St. Ward

(If death occurred in a hospital or institution, give its name instead of street and number)

2 FULL NAME R John McCarty

(a) Residence. No. 1108-22nd St. St. Ward

(b) Length of residence in city or town where death occurred 6 yrs. mos. ds. How long in U.S., if of foreign birth? yrs. mos. ds.

PERSONAL AND STATISTICAL PARTICULARS	MEDICAL CERTIFICATE OF DEATH
3 SEX 4 COLOR OR RACE 5 Single, Married, Widowed, or Divorced (write the word)	16 DATE OF DEATH (month, day and year)
Male White *Widower*	September 7th, 1926. 19

5a If married, widowed or divorced
HUSBAND of
(or) WIFE of

6 DATE OF BIRTH (month, day, and year)

17. I HEREBY CERTIFY, That I attended deceased from
19 to 19
that I last saw h alive on 19
and that death occurred, on the date stated above, at m.
The CAUSE OF DEATH* was as follows:

7 AGE			IF LESS than
Years	Months	Days	1 day, hrs.
75			or min.

Drown in bath tub *169*

Suicide

8 OCCUPATION OF DECEASED
(a) Trade, profession, or particular kind of work *Laborer*
(b) General nature of industry business. or establishment in which employed (or employer)
(c) Name of employer

(duration) yrs. mos. ds.
CONTRIBUTORY
(Secondary)

(duration) yrs. mos. ds.

9 BIRTHPLACE (city or town)
(State or country)

18 Where was disease contracted
if not at place of death?
Did an operation precede death? Date of
Was there an autopsy? *No*
What test confirmed diagnosis?
(Signed)

10 NAME OF FATHER

11 BIRTHPLACE OF FATHER
(City or town)
(State or country)

12 MAIDEN NAME OF MOTHER

13 BIRTHPLACE OF MOTHER
(City or town)
(State or country)

*State the Disease Causing Death, or in deaths from Violent Causes, state (1) Means and Nature of Injury, and (2) whether Accidental, Suicidal, or Homicidal. (See reverse side for additional space.)

14 Informant *Coroner's Office*
(Address)

19 PLACE OF BURIAL, CREMATION, OR REMOVAL *Riverside*   DATE OF BURIAL 9/11 19 26

Filed 9-11 1926 F M Leach Registrar.

20 UNDERTAKER *Rogers*   ADDRESS

THIS IS TO CERTIFY THAT THIS IS A TRUE AND CORRECT COPY OF THE OFFICIAL RECORD WHICH IS IN MY CUSTODY.

DATE ISSUED DEC 0 9 1997

LEE THIELEN
STATE REGISTRAR

SL
912636

Do not accept unless prepared on security paper with engraved border displaying the Colorado state seal and signature of the Registrar. PENALTY BY LAW, Section 25-2-118, Colorado Revised Statutes, 1982, if any person alters, uses, attempts to use or furnishes to another for deceptive use any vital statistics record. NOT VALID IF PHOTOCOPIED.

VR 50S 7/97

ANY ALTERATION OR ERASURE VOIDS THIS CERTIFICATE

State of Colorado death certificate for John McCarty.
Date of death: September 7, 1926.
Cause of death: suicide—drowned in bathtub.

59

References

Utah State Prison Records, Utah State Archives and Records Service, Salt Lake City, UT

United States Census, Ringgold County, Iowa 1860

Death Certificate of George McCarty, Oregon State Archives, Salem, OR

Death Certificate of Reatha McCarty Selig, Oregon State Archives, Salem, OR

Juab County Abstract Book, Levan, UT

Rand McNally's Pioneer Atlas of the American West, Copyright 1956, Library of Congress number 77-86939

History of Antimony, Chapter Two "Grass Valley Days," Chapter Three "Coyote Beginnings," Utah State Historical Society, Salt Lake City, UT

James H. Beckstad, Orem, UT

United States Census, Utah, 1880

Douglas County Archives, Roseburg, OR

Obituary of Nellie McCarty, *The Morning Democrat*, February 1, 1937, Baker, OR

History and Settlement of Northern San Juan County by Frank Silvey, Utah State Historical Society, Salt Lake City, UT

Tom McCarty's Own Story, notes by Charles Kelly, Preface by James Dullenty

Baker County Abstract Book, Baker, OR

East Oregonian, Pendleton, OR

History of Umatilla and Morrow Counties, W. H. Lever, Oregon State Prison Records

Oregon State Archives, Salem, OR

East Oregonian, Pendleton, OR, June 1893

Grand Junction News, November 12, 1887, Grand Junction, CO

Telluride Journal, June 1889, Telluride, CO

Bedrock Democrat, December 15-20, 1980, Baker, OR

The Wallowa Chieftain, October 8, 1891, Enterprise, OR

The Oregon Scout, November 4, 1891, Union. OR

The Oregon Scout, May 4, 1892, Union, OR

The Oregon Scout, May 5, 1892, Union, OR

The Bedrock Democrat, May, June and July 1892, Baker, OR

Oregon State Prison Records, Oregon State Archives, Salem, OR

History of Kittitas, Yakima and Klickitat Counties, 1904

Northern Kittitas County Tribune, Cle Elum, WA

The Wenatchee Daily World, Wenatchee, WA

Yakima Hearld Republic, Yakima, WA

Seattle Post-Intelligencer, Seattle, WA

Tacoma Daily Ledger, Tacoma, WA

The Morning Democrat, Baker, OR

East Oregonian, Pendleton, OR

The Oregonian, Portland, OR

The Great Roslyn Robbery, The Innocent were Arrested, Tried, Convicted, Dismissed. The Guilty were Arrested, Tried and Discharged. Austim Mires 1923. Published in The Record 1972, Volume 32 by Friends of the Library, Washington State University, Pullman, WA

The Bedrock Democrat, Baker, OR

Rocky Mountain News, March 30, 1889, Denver, CO

The Tacoma Daily Ledger, November 25, 1892, Tacoma, WA

The Delta Independent, September 13, 1893

East Oregonian, November 13, 1893, Pendleton, OR

East Oregonian, December 3, 1894, Pendleton, OR

Vernal Express, May 14, 1896, Vernal, UT

The Ogden Standard, May through September 17, 1896

The Messenger, July 10, 1896, Manti, UT

Eastern Utah Advocate, April 22, 1896, Price, UT

Eastern Utah Advocate, May 16, 1896, Price, UT

Bedrock Democrat, March 16, 1896, Baker, OR

The Weekly Republic, February 9, and 24, 1896, Union, OR

Laramie Daily Boomerang, Laramie, WY

Salt Lake Hearld, Salt Lake City, UT

Carbon County Journal, Rawlins, WY

Buffalo Bulletin, Buffalo, WY

Natrona County Tribune, Casper, WY,

Buffalo Voice, Buffalo, WY

Denver Daily News, Denver, CO, various dates from June 2 through September 1899.

The Wilcox Train Robbery, 1899, A Chronological Anaylsis by Emmett D. Chism.

Letter to Utah State Pardon Board from John T. McCarty, June 18, 1915

Eastern Utah Advocate, July 31, 1913, Price, UT and letter to Utah State Pardon Board, June 24, 1915

Utah State Prison Records, Utah State Archives and Records Service, Salt Lake City, UT

Death Certificate of John Thomas McCarty, State of Colorado and obituary in *Rocky Mountain News* September 7, 1926, Denver, CO

Deja Vu at Echo Cliffs

Most of southern Arizona is a hot, sandy desert covered by cactus. Most of northern Arizona is a beautiful, dry and elevated plateau. Green pines, firs and juniper trees growing in yellow to red-orange earth present a splendid picture. Interstate 40 originates in Chicago and ends in Los Angeles. Formerly it was called Route 66; before then it was a dirt road. And before that it was an Indian trail. Pacific Railroad tracks paralleled the road. At Seligman, Arizona, the tracks looped north to the town of Peach Springs and then went south to rejoin the road at Kingman.

In 1897, Abe Thompson lived in a cabin with his son about thirty-five miles north of Peach Springs. Jim Parker, Love "Kid" Marvin and Charles Douglass lived with the Thompsons. They were all rustlers and they burglarized neighboring homes when the owners were away. One day they decided to rob a train.

In the late evening of Monday, February 8, the Overland Santa Fe train was westbound to Los Angeles. Parker, Thompson and Douglass boarded the train east of Peach Springs. The train was approaching Rock Cut near Nelson when the bandits crawled over the coal tender, pulled on masks and pointed Colt revolvers at the engine crew. Parker told Engineer William Hase to stop the train; not having any real choice, he did as ordered. As the train slowly rolled to a stop, Douglass jumped off to uncouple the engine, coal tender, mail and express cars from the passenger cars. He fired a shot to announce a robbery in progress and to warn train crewmen to stay away.

Clerks Alexander Summers, Randall and Albert Grant in the express car noted and understood the unscheduled stop and pistol shot. Together they turned out their lights over their desks; Summers picked up his Colt .45 and Randall picked up his sawed-off 12-gauge shotgun. They opened the door slightly and saw Douglass uncoupling the cars.

Randall wanted to shoot Douglass, but Summers said no because he might be a brakeman. Randall then exited the side opposite Douglass and Summers the same side as Douglass, although further along the train. Summers stepped on the platform between cars; he saw Douglass looking at Randall. Douglass was raising his shotgun to fire and Summers took careful aim and fired. Douglass fell dead as Randall and Summers jumped off the train before it gained speed. Summers walked toward Douglass and fired two more shots in his body. Then he ordered Douglass to raise his hands. Douglass did not move, so Summers slowly approached and found that his first bullet had entered behind Douglass' left ear and exited his right eye. The other bullets were also mortal. Inspecting the corpse, Summers found dynamite and cigarettes. Summers called for help to find the other bandits. Randall was hiding in some brush and mail clerk Grant had stayed in the railroad car to hide the registered mail pouches under regular mail pouches. So Summers, Randall and a fireman walked two miles down the track to rejoin the train.

Engineer Hase stopped the train as ordered where Marvin was waiting with a team and wagon. Hase accompanied the bandits to the express car and was told to call out the clerks. He shouted for the clerks to open up or die. Clerk Grant opened the door and Parker entered. Parker couldn't blow the safe open because Douglass had been carrying the dynamite and he wasn't around. So Parker searched the registered mail and found nine packages that contained about $1,500 total. Disgusted, the bandits departed firing a few shots into the night air.

There had been some real excitement in the passenger cars. There was no reason for panic because the bandits never went near the passengers, but some passengers became hysterical. One overweight woman wore expensive jewelry and she became uncontrollable. She tried to unbutton her dress at the bodice in order to hide her valuables in that intimate part of her anatomy. Her fingers wouldn't function so she asked a nearby gentleman to do the honors. Working closely together, they hid her valuables.

Sheriffs of Yavapai, Mojave and Cococino counties were notified by telegraph. Sheriff Fletcher Fairchild, by chance, was in Peach Springs and immediately organized a small posse. Fairchild took volunteers looking for excitement or a quick reward, not experienced lawmen. He hired some Walapai Indians to track the bandits. Leaving early Tuesday morning, they found a trail a few miles east of Peach Springs. Early in the evening Fairchild was riding far in advance of the posse and spotted Parker. Parker was mounted on a well-known race horse that he had stolen. Shots were exchanged at long range and Fairchild pressed on steadily. Parker would take cover and fire shots then race to more cover and shoot again. Fairchild recognized the bandit as Jim Parker, a local tough who would steal anything of value. At dark Parker disappeared behind a ridge near the road from Peach Springs to Grand Canyon.

The trail was lost near Music Mountain and Milkweed Springs. At this time the Indians left saying that they had urgent business elsewhere. The posse refused to continue, so they all returned to Peach Springs.

Arriving back at Peach Springs, Fairchild was delighted to find experienced manhunters forming a new posse. Sheriffs Cameron and Ruffner, deputies Bayless, Bugglin and Munds plus U.S. Marshall Morrell were all there. John Rogers, recently released from the county jail, volunteered to go along.

Wednesday morning the posse followed the trail to Abe Thompson's cabin. Here they found the race horse and saddle Parker had discarded. They also found lots of supplies. Evidently the bandits had planned to pack the supplies and ride into Utah. With the death of Douglass, Thompson and Marvin went to Peach Springs to lounge around and Parker decided to move north. He wrapped his feet in blankets. This was to confuse the trackers into thinking the footprints he made were from Indian moccasins. The trackers found his discarded boots and weren't confused for a minute. All day the posse followed the trail. It reached about 6,500-feet elevation; snow lay in shady spots and on north slopes. The trail led fifteen miles northwest then turned southwest for about twenty-five miles. Here Parker came to a point on Diamond Creek nine miles north of Peach Springs. He circled back to set up an ambush overlooking his back trail. He waited but the posse didn't come.

Thursday morning Parker left his ambush site, discarding another pair of boots and an overcoat. He walked up Diamond Creek all day then circled back to another ambush site. Still, the posse didn't show.

Friday morning Parker again followed Diamond Creek after throwing away another overcoat. He reached Grand Canyon that evening and the posse was six hours behind. Parker had given up walking on rocks to hide his tracks. He was now walking in the middle of the road leaving an easy trail to follow. The posse was often delayed because they correctly interpreted the ambush sites and were very cautious when approaching open areas without cover. That night the posse camped in a cabin on Diamond Creek, a mile from the Colorado River.

Saturday morning at dawn the Mojave trackers and John Rogers moved out. Soon they saw Parker far ahead moving down the Colorado River. They followed him for fifteen miles before they caught up to him. Four cocked Winchester rifles were pointed at Parker who saw the wisdom in surrendering. As it was close to dark, they decided not to start back. They built a fire and waited for morning. Sometime during the night all four captors fell asleep but Parker didn't. He grabbed a Winchester and fired, scattering the Indians and Rogers. Parker then reversed his course and walked up the Colorado River toward Diamond Creek Canyon. The Indians went straight to the posse's camp and related the capture and escape. Then they quit the chase and went home.

Sunday morning Sheriff Cameron raced for Peach Springs to telegraph other lawmen to watch the lower Colorado River. His posse was to search Diamond Creek Canyon.

Monday morning Sheriff Ruffner and deputies Martin Bugglin and Will Riley were moving down Diamond Creek Canyon and saw Parker wading upstream in Diamond Creek. They hid and waited. Parker walked into the trap and Ruffner shouted for him to drop his rifle and surrender. Parker raised his rifle and Bugglin and Riley fired over his head. Parker then surrendered. He was covered with blisters and his feet were frostbitten. He said he hadn't eaten in fifty hours. They reached Peach Springs at 7:30 P.M. The sheriff arrested Abe Thompson and Kid Marvin. John Rogers was also arrested for aiding a fugitive to escape. He had previously been implicated in suspicious dealings with Parker. Charles Douglass was buried, but his clothing was held as evidence. He died wearing a two-pants suit stolen from Ayer's Ranch. (A two-pants suit was a jacket and two matching pairs of pants. The reason for two pairs of pants was that pants wore out twice as fast as the jacket, therefore all three would wear out at the same time.) One pair of pants was on Douglass and the other pair was found at his cabin. Dynamite, fuses and blasting caps were also discovered. Marvin had bought some cartridges at a store and the clerk recognized the price markings as his handwriting.

At that very point in time the U.S. Congress was studying a bill to make train robbing a capital offense. In the previous six years, 186 trains had been stopped for criminal purposes. This resulted in 75 deaths and 58 citizens wounded by gunfire. It was not passed into law.

March and April brought a beautiful spring to the high country. Birds sang on Music Mountain as wild flowers bent to gentle, warm breezes. The snow was gone and new life appeared to enjoy the marvels of a full life.

Parker and five other prisoners in Prescott's jail were not enjoying the season's beauty and bounty in their austere confines. Instead they studied their captors' habits. The deputies went home for lunch at noon. Sheriff Ruffner also left at noon for lunch and stopped by the stable to attend to his favorite horse before returning shortly after 1 P.M.

On Sunday, May 9th, circumstances were just right. About 1 P.M., jailer Meador responded to a prisoner's request for a bucket of water. The jail did not have modern plumbing thus requiring that water buckets be filled at the jail well. Meador filled the bucket and placed it just outside the corridor door. As Meador opened the corridor door, Cornelia, a Mexican prisoner, stepped out to take the bucket back into the jail and attacked Meador. Parker and forger L. C. Miller ran past the struggling pair to arm themselves with revolvers and a shotgun. Meador yelled for help and Deputy District Attorney Lee Norris rushed downstairs from his office on the second floor. Norris saw Parker aim the shotgun at him so he quickly turned around to climb the stairs. Parker fired and Norris was mortally wounded. Cornelia finally overpowered Meador by striking his head with the heavy jail keys. It was an ugly scalp wound that bled freely. The three escapees ran outside to enter the stable. Meador fired three shots at them. Later he told the sheriff that he thought he missed all three times. He was wrong.

The three entered the stable and Parker not seeing the sheriff demanded to know where he was. The stable man did not know and said so. Unbeknownst to either, the sheriff had gone on business to Congress (a small town) about forty miles south. Parker was furious as he had planned to kill the sheriff at the stable. Taking some guns, Parker mounted the sheriff's favorite horse bareback. Cornelia and Miller rode double bareback on another horse. By this time a crowd of fifty people had gathered to investigate the shots. Police Chief Archibald was among them. Not one citizen could do anything to stop them as none were armed. The escapees rode south out of town. A posse soon formed and the local militia furnished old surplus .45-70 Springfield army rifles and ammunition. They left an hour behind the fugitives.

Sheriff Ruffner arrived back about 7 P.M. He telegraphed lawmen at Crowned King and Chaparral to be alert. He offered a $1,000 reward, dead or alive, for the escapees.

Deputies Munds and Yoomans, leading a small posse, approached Beck's Ranch on Lynx Creek. Parker and Miller were there and fired on the posse. Returning gunfire wounded Miller who crawled to the bush that Parker was hiding behind. Miller stood up and raised his hands surrendering. Parker cursed him for cowardice and lack of nerve. Parker mounted the horse and pulled Miller up behind him and they rode off into the darkness dodging bullets. They rode toward the Aqua Fria Valley where they hoped to steal horses.

Lee Norris died just before midnight. His last statement was that either Miller or Parker shot him. He was highly regarded and everyone liked him. He was eulogized eloquently as a fine man of sterling virtues and devotion to his fellow man with high principles. Locals talked of having Judge Lynch hear the case and mandating the ultimate final punishment.

The posse was on the trail at dawn. They found where the sheriff's horse threw a shoe. It had a habit of going lame quickly without a shoe. The horse was never seen again.

Deputy Fletcher Fairchild was a dedicated lawman. He was smart and had an excellent memory. He teamed up with railroad detective Cade Selvey and they rode into the Tonto Basin. Rumor had it that Parker was there, but they were just that—rumors. Not finding their quarry, Fairchild remembered that Miller had a relative in Jerome. Fairchild contacted the relative and convinced him that if Miller surrendered to him he would be taken to Flagstaff. If Prescott people got hold of him they would lynch him. Fairchild was convincing and was led to Miller's hiding place two miles from Jerome. Miller was glad to surrender as he had been wounded twice. Meador's bullet had found the mark, however it wasn't serious.

Miller talked freely saying that Cornelia and Parker had also been wounded by Meador. He said six jailbirds were involved in plotting the escape. They wanted to go upstairs and rob the county treasury and agreed to shoot anyone who interfered.

Miller was locked up in Flagstaff on May 15th, a Saturday. A week from the following Tuesday some ninety miles north at Willow Springs, Parker knocked on the door of Campbell and Preston's Trading Post. S. S. Preston let him in and Parker sat by the fire while he waited for breakfast to cook. He was nervous and bought canned fruit and chewing tobacco. Preston was almost positive that this man was Parker. They exchanged views on recent news. Parker said he was looking for some stolen horses and that he hadn't eaten for five days. He asked about the road north, trails and springs. Parker paid his bill and left at 7 A.M. Preston immediately rode to Tuba City about twelve miles east for a detailed description from deputies. Finding only one deputy, he confirmed his suspicions by examining Parker's description.

Preston returned to his trading post and hired nine Navajos, at $15 each, to track Parker. It was late in the afternoon before they got started. The trackers and Preston did not stop at dark. They rode all night covering about fifty miles. At the foot of Echo Cliffs they came upon Parker's camp just at dawn. His horse was picketed nearby and they surrounded him. Parker was asleep so one shot was fired. Parker sat up with a Winchester ready.

"Is that you Fletch?" Parker inquired, obviously expecting Deputy Fairchild.

"You lay that gun down and come up here," Preston replied.

"You come down here." Parker answered.

Then Preston declared, "You get up here or be killed."

Parker dropped his weapon and walked up to Preston and the Navajos. Preston searched his prisoner and the party started back to Willow Springs. They arrived there about 1 P.M. and rested till 5 P.M. Then they rode toward Flagstaff and camped by the Little Colorado River. Before dawn Sheriff Ruffner and Deputy Fairchild arrived to take charge of the prisoner.

Sheriff Ruffner and Deputy Fairchild returned Miller and Parker to Prescott. They rode the train but not to the Prescott depot. The sheriff had arranged to get off at Wipple and ride carriages to the jail at midnight. About 200 people were waiting at the jail when the group arrived. Some threats were made and Miller nearly panicked but Parker cursed him. The crowd demanded the prisoners but the sheriff refused. The crowd then dispersed and the prisoners were lodged in cells.

Parker boasted that he would not attend the trial. He said that he had retrieved the $1,500 from the train robbery and had spent it. He had been free fifteen days. Records disclosed that Parker was from Tulare County, California, and had served two short terms in San Quentin. He moved to Arizona about 1891. His parents were well-respected people but his mother had died when he was five. His father went insane when he was fifteen. He had two sisters and their grandfather raised them. The family was heartbroken about his lifestyle.

The short trial started June 17th. The jury was out thirty minutes. Miller was found guilty and one juror would not vote to hang him, so he received life in Yuma. Judge Hawkins after pronouncing sentence had a few words for Miller.

"In your case, Miller, I desire to further say that it is hoped that Arizona may never be cursed with a chief executive who will exercise any clemency in your behalf." Miller obviously was shaken at these words. Parker never flinched and looked the judge squarely in both eyes as he was sentenced to hang. Abe Thompson received five years in Yuma Prison. Marvin and Rogers were not prosecuted. Cornelia was last seen by old Fort McDowell headed for Mexico.

The sentence was appealed but the following February it was affirmed. Parker bet the sheriff he wouldn't hang. His demeanor changed radically. He had been morose and sullen. Then he started yelling and picking up imaginary objects from the floor. Clearly he was feigning insanity. At times he was almost normal.

On June 3, 1898, Parker was in good spirits and ate a hearty breakfast. Father Quetu had just baptized him and accepted him into the Catholic Church. He was led out to the east of the court house to a small enclosure. Inside was a black scaffold. Parker examined it thoroughly and expressed his satisfaction. He climbed the steps then did a few dance steps before removing his slippers. Sheriff Ruffner asked him for any last words. Parker shook hands with all present and said, "I won't disappoint you, I'll die game." Obviously this took some courage and strength of character. The trapdoor opened at 10:31 A.M. and he was dead in ten minutes and forty-five seconds. He was cut down four minutes later. His neck had been broken.

Sheriff Ruffner paid all rewards and expenses out of his own purse. It seems paradoxical that Sheriff Ruffner sent Thompson's son to Mojave County for them to provide for till Thompson's release.

References

Cococino Sun, Flagstaff, AR
Prescott Morning Courier, Prescott, AR
Sharlot Hall/Prescott Historical Society, Prescott, AR

Breaking the Convict Code

The California State Prison at Folsom is on the east bank of the American River. It is about twenty miles east and south of Sacramento, the state capital. It was built of rock quarried on the site by convict labor. Occupying three levels of the canyon wall, the site was poorly chosen. The cell blocks and ancillary buildings were built first. The walls were completed after forty-three years of hard work in 1923. In 1903 there were few buildings, and lacking walls, low fences and deadlines were used to contain the inmate population. Deadlines usually resembled the white line on a baseball diamond. The inmates knew if they crossed them, they would be shot by sharpshooting guards. The guards shot to kill and convicts died trying to escape. There were permanent and temporary guard towers strategically placed to oversee cons at their work sites.

Warden Thomas Wilkinson was a political hack appointed as a reward for loyalty to the Democratic party. Not being an experienced penologist, he was occasionally manipulated by clever convict influence. He had been quoted as saying that he would rather take the word of his "pet" convict Raymond than the oath of any of his guards.

Convict John H. Wood, prison number 5090, hated Folsom from the day he arrived there in January of 1902. He conspired about an escape with Joe Murphy, #5324, a burglar from Contra Costa County and Wood's regiment buddy from the Spanish-American War, and several others he thought he could trust. He determined that the only way to escape was to launch simultaneous attacks on a fellow named Chalmers, keeper at the east gate, and hold it open till the attack on the captain's office was successful in taking hostages. With hostages and an open gate, the

71

San Francisco Call, Dec. 9, 1901.

FOOTPAD STOPS THE WRONG MAN

Philip Krell Holds Up the Man Who Tries to Rob Him.

Philip Krell, a showcase maker, held up a footpad who tried to serve him the same trick about 11:30 o'clock last night at Pine and Sansome streets.

The encounter occurred a few minutes after the intended victim had finished a satisfying meal at a nearby restaurant and was strolling homeward, satisfied with himself and all the world. Suddenly, out of the darkness, the figure of a man loomed and sharp came the command, emphasized with a pointed revolver, to halt. The unoccupied hand of the highwayman was plunged into the showcase maker's pocket and came forth with a watch.

Krell does not know why he did it, but he did. He reached for the footpad, grabbing both his hands, the one that held the weapon and the other holding the watch. The holdup struggled to get free and made several attempts to turn the revolver on his captor, but did not succeed.

Krell held to his man and yelled for help. It came in the persons of Policemen Leonard and Farrell. As they approached, the footpad threw into the street the revolver and the watch, which were picked up by the policemen after they had taken him off Krell's hands.

At the City Prison, where the footpad was booked for robbery, he gave his name as Frank Graham. He says he is a laborer and came here several days ago from Arkansas. He is twenty-four years old.

GET LONG TER IN PRISON

Judges Sentence T Men Convicted o Crime.

JOHN H. WOOD, alias **FRANK HAM**, thirty years of age, lif prisonment in Folsom for hig robbery.

CHARLES NELSON, thirty-five of age, twenty-seven years in Quentin for highway robbery.

ANTONE M'DONALD, sixty-s ears old, ten years in San Que r grand larceny.

John H. Wood, alias Frank Graham ore Superior Judge Cook yest sentence for the robbery of Philip the night of December 8th at Pin some streets.

Something must be done," said the C check the inclination of the semi-w element in the city to turn foot n pressed by wants often brought o us living. The best remedy for s long sentences." He conclude Woods' term at life in Folsom Pr at's a pretty tough deal," said er, affecting a look of unconcern down. Woods was formerly a so w service in the Philippines

nce of twenty-seven years' imp t in San Quentin for highway as imposed upon Charles Nelson r Judge Dunne. Nelson's par e, Edward Davis, will be dealt w rning. Nelson and Davis stop Hamlin and Otto Fleissner, org e First Presbyterian Church, at f Jackson street and Van Ness s the evening of November 2d l eaded guilty, but Davis stood t convicted.

McDonald, who gave his age n years, was also sentenced ne to ten years' imprisonment in for grand larceny.

San Francisco Call, Jan. 25, 190

escapees could blow open the armory and secure firearms—then into the hills to freedom.

The biggest obstacle to this plan was guard Joseph Prigmore. There were other guards, including Betz, Anderson, Cann, Eveland and Luttrel; but Prigmore was the most feared and respected tower guard at Folsom. It was a well-earned reputation. He was an expert shot with a strong resolve to shoot when necessary. He had proven this several times. On June 25, 1893, several cons had former convict Fredrickson hide guns in the rock quarry at night. On June 27, the cons grabbed the weapons and took Lt. Briar hostage and started toward freedom. Prigmore shouted from his tower to stop or he would shoot to kill. They didn't and he did. Prigmore killed convicts Wilson, Dalton and "Smiling Frank Williams." Then he opened up with his Gatling gun and wounded Sontag and Ira Abbott. Years later he shot convict Carl Weber as he tried to swim across the river. When Charles Aull was warden, he told Prigmore that whenever he saw a break he was to stop it.

"Shoot regardless if they have hostages because it is a lot better that I or other prison officials die than let a lot of desperate men out to kill or outrage the public." Aull died in the fall of 1899 of natural causes and Wilkinson replaced him.

All guards were required to target practice; convict Ira Abbott was the score keeper. Thus, he knew who shot the best. The escape conspirators discussed the information and decided that Prigmore and others must go if they were to succeed. So "pet" Raymond convinced Warden Wilkinson to fire Prigmore. Prigmore was fired because he wrote a letter to his cousin, a guard at San Quentin, describing customs and conditions at Folsom. He denied writing it; it was undoubtedly a clever forgery written by a convict. The letter was published in the *San Francisco Examiner*. Prigmore and the *San Francisco Examiner* editor swore that Prigmore was not the author of the letter. Guards Eveland, Nickerson, Anderson, Betz and Luttrel were all fired for minor complaints, not neglect of duty.

In Folsom, just as in any prison, there were informants. One such snitch, stool pigeon or rat was convict D. B. Rogers. He

CONVICTS KNEW HE WOULD SHOOT TO KILL; HE WAS DISCHARGED

Joseph Prigmore, Who Was a Terror to the Felons at Folsom, Dismissed From Service by Warden Wilkinson.

In discussing the recent break at Folsom Prison, when thirteen convicts managed to effect their escape, a gentleman who is thoroughly conversant with prison affairs at Folsom said: "The greatest mistake made by Warden Wilkinson during his administration was the discharge of such old experienced guards as Joe Prigmore, Tom Betz, Anderson, Cann and others.

It Would Have Been Different.

"Had Prigmore been on the armory post that morning none of these convicts would be at liberty and the chances are that many of them would have been under the sod. This last break recalls the break engineered by George Sontag, which took place June 27, 1903, when the convicts captured Lieutenant Frank Brier of the prison guard force and attempted to rush him through the lines.

"In that case the convicts found, to their cost, that they had to deal with a man who was not afraid to perform his duty and the result was that three of them were killed, and four others wounded, and the break was prevented. Prigmore was discharged by Warden Wilkinson on the excuse that he was giving information about prison matters to the public press.

Prigmore Had to Go.

"One of the San Francisco dailies published an article criticising Warden Wilkinson's methods, and that of-

surface and that was the last that was ever seen of him.

Charley Aull's Way.

"When Charley Aull was Warden, he called me into his office and said: 'Mr. Prigmore, whenever you see the convicts attempting to make a break, I want you to stop them. Shoot, no matter if they have me or any of the other of the prison officials in their custody. Be as careful as you can not to hit the free men, but shoot just the same whenever you get half a chance, for it is better that I or any of the other officials be killed than to have a lot of these desperate men running around the country who will, perhaps, kill and outrage innocent people. We are paid to take such chances.' You would never have heard Warden Aull giving instructions not to shoot, under circumstances like those recently seen at Folsom. He would have yelled 'shoot,' and would have discharged the guard who failed to obey his instructions.

"Always in the Way."

"I also had a chance to shoot in the attempted break made on the other side of the river in March, 1894, when Convict Garcia was shot in the arm, and Convict Turner was shot through the side. I don't know whether I got those men or Guard Ellis got them, as we were both shooting at them and they were 300 yards away from my post. I had several other chances to shoot at convicts during the nine years that I served as guard at Folsom, as it seemed that I was always in the way when a break or an escape was at-

The Sacramento Union, Aug. 10, 1903.

learned of the plot and told chief turnkey (guard) P. J. Cochrane. Cochrane did not give much credibility to the information. "Oh, give us something new," he told Rogers. Again on the morning of July 27, 1903, Rogers said, "It's coming." Cochrane in casual conversation with Captain Murphy mentioned it. Murphy acknowledged that he had heard of the escape plot. They were too late to stop it.

Monday the 27th was a normal work day, so cons were released from their cells and ate breakfast. As usual, they left the mess hall casually to smoke and gossip while drifting into their respective work lines. As the lines formed, Warden Wilkinson; his nephew Harry, a stenographer; Captain R. J. Murphy; quarry boss G. E. Jeter; guards Joe Klenzendorf, C. H. Jolly, W. J. Hopton and Lauren Ventrees; T. C. Brown, ambulance driver; chief engineer C. H. Ward; and general overseer McDonough gathered in the captain's office. They had assembled there to hold a typical court session. Any rule infraction lodged by a guard against a convict was investigated and adjudicated. That was a lot of people in a fifteen-by-fifteen-foot room.

The east gate was really a sally port. A sally port is two consecutive gates on a common road, the distance apart determined by the length of a four-horse team and wagon. For a wagon to exit, the inner gate was opened, the wagon driven in and stopped and the gate closed. The wagon would then be searched for escapees, following that the outer gate would be opened and the wagon would exit the prison. A pedestrian sally port operated similarly adjacent to the wagon sally port. A Gatling gun was located directly above the sally ports.

At 8 A.M. most of the Upper Yard Line had been passed through the gate to their workplaces and the Stone Line was almost out. Some 380 convicts still remained in the Garden Line, Stable Line and Dairy Line. Suddenly several cons rushed out of line and into the captain's office. They were armed with prison-made knives and straight razors. They ordered the staff members to form two lines and the cons formed a line in between for protection from gunfire. The hostages were ordered to march to the sally port or die.

No. 5720
Name Harry Eldridge
County Sacramento
Crime Murder 1st Degree
Term Death   years.
Received June 4" 1904
Discharged
Remarks 5 Icon

No. 5090
Name John H. Wood.
County San Francisco
Crime Robbery
Term Life   year
Received Jan 27. 1902
Discharged
Remarks

No. 4228
Name Fred Howard
County Sacramento.
Crime Robbery.
Term ___ 15 ___ years.
Received Nov. 17. 1897
Discharged Apl. 17. 1907
Remarks:

No. 5099   3+.
Name Frank Case
County Los Angeles.
Crime Robbery.
Term ___ Life ___ years.
Received Feb. 9. 1902
Discharged

No. 5096
Name Ed. Davis
County San Francisco.
Crime Robbery.
Term ___ 33 ___ years.
Received Jan 31. 1902
Discharged Dec. 31. 1921
Remarks

No. 4967   37.
Name Ray Fahey.
County Sacramento.
Crime Robbery -
Term Life :   years.
Received July 29.01
Discharged
Remarks

No. 5135.
Name Jas Roberts.
County San Francisco.
Crime Robbery.
Term — 20 —   years.
Received April 6.1902
Discharged Aug 6.1914
Remarks

No. 4748   27.
Name R. M. Gordon.
County Sacramento.
Crime Robbery.
Term — 45 —   years.
Received Feb. 23.1900
Discharged Jan. 23.1927
Remarks:

No. 5201
Name John Joseph Allison
County San Joaquin
Crime Robt + Burg. 2nd deg (2 cts)
Term 4   years.
Received January 7 - 1903
Discharged January 7 - 1906

No. 4810
Name A. Seavis
County Sacramento
Crime Robbery
Term — 25 — years.
Received Aug. 8. 1900
Discharged Nov. 8. 1915
Remarks:

No. 5358
Name Frank Miller
County Fresno
Crime Burg. 1st Deg
Term Twelve (12) years.
Received April 25th 1903
Discharged Dec. 25th 1910.
Remarks

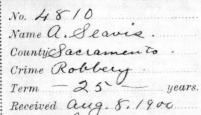

No. 5324
Name Joseph Murphy
County Contra Costa
Crime Burg. 1st Deg.
Term 14 years.
Received February 26th 1903
Discharged November 26th 1911

No. 3913
Name Wm. Lavonne
County Madera
Crime Robbery
Term 45 years.
Received Sept. 23 - 96
Discharged Aug. 23 - 1923
Remarks:
2d Term

Simultaneously, convicts Myers and Leverone, who were in the sally port, attacked gate keeper Chalmers. Chalmers was cut on his hand and two convicts rushed to his aid. Together they pushed the attackers back into the yard and secured the gate. Chief turnkey Cochrane was nearby and saw the attack at the sally port was over so he rushed into the captain's office. He went in swinging his cane and a real donnybrook started.

Guard Cotter was slashed across the stomach and disemboweled. He fell saying he was done for. Guard Jolly and Cochrane were stabbed repeatedly. Captain Murphy tried to run out the rear door to throw away the yard keys but was stopped. A con finally broke a chair over Cochrane's head and the fight was over. Two lines of hostages protected the inner line of cons as they marched to the sally port. The warden ordered the gate opened and reluctantly it was. Approaching the armory door, convict Roberts was preparing his dynamite charge to open the door. The warden was persuaded to order it opened upon being threatened with death. The door was opened and cons rushed in to take ten Winchester repeating rifles and twenty-five Colt revolvers plus ammunition. Then the large group moved east and over the hill. As they passed guards houses, Klenzendorf saw his wife and children wave at him. He wondered if he would ever see them again. Just over the hill the warden, being overweight, was out of breath and had to stop. He was robbed of his clothing and valuables, returning to the prison in his underwear. Hostages had been carrying Jolly and Cochrane, as both were severely wounded. Cochrane and Jolly were thrown in a ditch. The group moved east to the Mormon Island Bridge. Guard Ryan had followed the group and fired at long range. This shot caused some confusion and Guard Ventrees grabbed a dropped revolver and jumped into the river and hid.

Back at the prison some 380 convicts were still in line and wondering if they should have joined the escapees. Myers and Leverone were locked in the dungeon. They cursed their co-conspirators who failed to aid them in their assault on Chalmers. All cons were locked up and counted. Twenty-five guards left in horse drawn busses in pursuit. The prison could not operate with such a reduced staff so the cons stayed in their cells. They

Folsom Prison, interior cell building.

Photo: California State Library

Folsom Prison, looking north.

Folsom Prison, stone quarry.

enjoyed several days' vacation from work. Only a few trustees were let out to do necessary chores like feeding the animals and watering the gardens, etc.

There were thirteen escapees: Fred Howard, R. M. Gordon, A. Seavus, Ray Fahey, John H. Wood, Frank Case, Ed Davis, James Roberts, John J. Allison, Frank Miller, Joe Murphy, Harry Eldridge and Joseph Theron.

The news spread. Sheriffs of Sacramento, El Dorado, Placer, Amador, Yolo, Yuba and San Joaquin Counties formed posses. Governor Pardee activated C and H Companies of the National Guard. A small Sanitary Corps group volunteered under the direction of Dr. H. H. Look.

As the cons and hostages moved east, they came upon Joe Foster with his four-horse team and wagon load of wood. Another man, Ben Schlotman, chanced by and together they were ordered to unload the wood. Then the cons rode in the wagon with the hostages walking alongside. The cons expected an encounter at every turn in the road. They moved slowly and cautiously arriving at Pilot Hill, about eighteen miles from Folsom, around 3 P.M. The cons looted S. D. Diehl's store of tobacco, provisions and whiskey. They ate at the hotel. Then they lounged around waiting for the 5 P.M. stagecoach. Arriving on time, the driver was asked if he had seen a posse. He answered no as did chance travelers from the opposite direction. Loading up the wagon and assuming their previous positions all moved east. Convict Wood was the obvious leader and he announced that the hostages would be released soon. It was welcome news.

However, unbeknownst to the group, a posse was waiting in ambush close by. A convict accidentally fired his revolver and the posse thought it was discovered. So they fired a volley and con J. J. Allison was struck in his chest. He fell to the wagon bed knowing that his wound was mortal. He put his revolver to his head and ended his life. Deputy Hinters shot the wheel horse and that immobilized the wagon. A white flag was raised and the three lines formed again and the group walked east. About four miles down the road at 10 P.M. Wood spoke to the hostages.

"Boys you can go now. Goodbye and good luck."

83

The hostages started back quickly but became confused in the dark. So they sat under a tree till dawn. The cons scattered into the brush. Actually, this was a brilliant decision because to effectively guard the hostages would have required a large fire all night for illumination. That would have pinpointed their location to a posse. Clearly the hostages had outworn their usefulness.

The next morning Allison was buried where he died. A deputy dug out the bullet and displayed it on the wall of the sheriff's office for years.

The surrounding area was low rolling hills densely covered with brush and scrub oak trees. These were the foothills of the mighty Sierra Nevada Mountains. Dusty trails crisscrossed in circles or went nowhere. A man could easily hide ten feet from another. Mounted posses patrolled the road and passable trails in daylight. They followed footprints of convicts because P was imprinted on the sole of their shoes.

Saturday night just before dusk, members of Company H were following some prints at the foot of a hill. Lieutenant Smith and five others took up positions at the dry creek bed. Six guardsmen were to evenly space themselves apart and walk abreast on the hilltop and move down hill to the others. Before reaching the hilltop shots rang out and Festus Rutherford and Charles Jones were killed. The remaining posse members regrouped with Lieutenant Smith. Fifty to seventy shots were fired. The guardsmen at the creek bed could not see anything to shoot at. Reinforcements were sent for. Sheriff Bosquit responded and decided to set fire to the brush hoping to flush out the culprits. As dry as that brush was, the only way to stop such a fire was to wait for winter snow. The sheriff relented.

Early in the morning the cons were gone but the guardsmen's bodies were found. Rutherford was shot through the abdomen and had two leg wounds. Jones lay face down and the cons had emptied their guns into his body. The sad procession walked slowly by the Grand Victory Mine on their way to Placerville with the bodies. On August fourth Major Simonds assembled the sixty-five-strong H Company to hear Reverend George C. King

Festus Rutherford and Charles Jones Fa
Before the Rifles of Fugitive Felons.

Both Were Members of Company H, N. G. C., of Placerville, and They Died Bravely in Discharge of Duty—The Refugees Are Surrounded Near Placerville, and a Battle is Expected at Daylight This Morning.

PLACERVILLE, August 1.—The desperate thugs who escaped from the Folsom State Prison last Monday have added two more victims to their list of murders by slaying Festus Rutherford and Charles Jones, who were of the pursuing party. They also wounded James Gill.

The men are at bay in the underbrush on a hill near Placerville and are surrounded by 150 men who will make an attack on them at daylight.

William Gill, a deaf man, resident of Placerville, went out to help in the man-hunt. While passing along the road he was called on to halt, and not hearing the challenge, he kept on his way and was shot and killed.

house, where the convicts appear noon."

How Henry Walters Saw It—Da of Shooting Friends.

When Henry Walters had coll himself he was able to tell his sto

"We had been at the foot of th vine only a few minutes," he said, our boys had almost reached the mit, when the shooting commence the bullets came fast. We could n the fight because of the brush.

"It was a trying situation for the foot of the hill. The bullets humming around us, but we cou no shooting. We might have h soldiers instead of the convicts.

"Then one of the men in khak form emerged from the brush u hill and called out to us to ru doctors and reinforcements."

FIVE CONVICTS IN BAN
And the Attacking Militiamen But Six In Number.

PLACERVILLE, Aug. 1.—A c ate fight between a band of five escaped Folsom convicts and a of six militiamen who were follo fresh trail of the convicts, took this evening, just at dusk, on a near the Grand Victory mine, a result of the conflict two of tl tiamen named Festus Rutherf

Sacramento Bee, August 1, 1903.

deliver the eulogies. Flags flew at half-staff and all local businesses were closed on the fifth.

Meanwhile, the cons had split into three groups. Governor Pardee offered an additional $500 reward to the standard $50 for the return of any escapee. The foothills were in turmoil. Hundreds of men, organized and disorganized, roamed the area. Bloodhounds were brought in from Reno, Nevada. Rumors were persistent that all of the convicts were opium addicts and they would surrender when their supplies of opium ran out. One evening a Placerville resident was walking along a road and came upon a posse. Posse members shouted for him to halt but he did not stop and he was shot dead. He was deaf.

Convicts Howard, Roberts and Fahey followed the American River west toward Sacramento. On August 6 they were in the rail yards after dark. Sacramento Police Detective Michael Fisher and Deputy Wittenbrock were searching the rail yards. Their flashlight beam discovered Fahey; Fisher instantly recognized him and started shooting. Fahey and his partner returned fire and slipped away in the night.

In Auburn, Sheriff Keena and Deputy Coan were alerted that Seavus, the only African-American escapee, had been seen boarding train 214 in Newcastle. When train 214 arrived, the lawmen walked slowly down both sides of the cars and soon spotted Seavus. They called upon him to surrender and he answered with pistol shots. The lawmen returned fire with shotguns, wounding Seavus in his legs. He surrendered and his wounds were treated. Originally Seavus had been arrested in Sacramento's Chinatown for vagrancy. When he was searched, police found a stolen watch and four dollars. He was sentenced to Folsom for twenty-five years.

Seavus had been very active during the escape and threatened to kill all of the hostages several times. The others convinced him not to. He had left the group with Case, Davis, Roberts and Fahey. (Case, a convict with a history of minor crimes, was in Folsom after committing robbery and beating up a man.) One night Seavus and Case came upon a cabin. Approaching it, they were greeted with gunfire and returned fire. They ran up a brushy hill and Case fell down. So Seavus hid close by and watched Case for half an hour. Case did not move so he probably was dead. He was never seen again.

That same night five cons were eating supper at James Hawkins ranch near Omo. Departing peaceably, they went toward the Consumnes River. Phillip Springer, a local citizen, was walking along a road near Placerville. Posse members C. L. Westlake and William Blake shot and killed him. Another innocent victim.

Ex-convict William Neuman was walking along the railroad tracks west of Sacramento and met escapees Roberts and Howard. Being well acquainted, they exchanged the pleasantries of the day and recent events. Arriving in Davisville, Neuman excused himself saying he had agreed to clean a stable. Instead he went straight to the sheriff's office and informed on his friends. Deputies were dispatched to the area. Moving in a skirmish line (spread out and moving as a line abreast across an area), they flushed out several men from brushy Putah Creek. Near a cabin Roberts appeared and Sacramento County Deputy Sheriff Hinters shouted, "Get up your hands or I'll plug you."

Roberts hands went up and Hinters said, "Hello Roberts, caught at last, eh?"

Roberts replied, "It's all off, gentlemen, I'm an escaped convict and you've got me, but I made a good run for it."

Hinters gave him a stiff drink of whiskey and Roberts talked freely. Roberts was interviewed the next day by a newspaper reporter. Roberts was undoubtedly the proudest man in California after being told that the crowd gathered to see him at the depot was bigger than the crowd that saw President Roosevelt there. He smiled condescendingly as if to say "why sure, and why not?" His ego was overwhelming. He bragged that he would go to the gallows without flinching, as he fully expected to be hanged.

A woman by the name of Palmer lived about four miles west of Davisville and reported seeing a suspicious character loitering near her farm. Yolo County Deputies Johnson and Hainline hurried to the farm. Arriving there they saw a man bathing in Putah Creek. Simultaneously, he saw two armed men with badges, so he grabbed his clothing and ran. He ignored an order to halt, so both deputies fired, breaking both of his arms. He kept running and the deputies fired again mortally wounding him. He had been dressed in a striped shirt and overalls and his shoes were two sizes too big for his feet. He had a Colt revolver in his bundle. He had only been in the area two days and people who spoke to him thought him deranged. He had no identification, so he was photographed and pictures were sent to Folsom and San Quentin for possible identification. Prison officials could not identify him so he was buried unknown.

On August 16 four escapees appeared at Glen Alpine Resort and ate a hearty meal. They took food with them and left without incident.

Sunday night, August 23, Joe Murphy and Frank Miller, walked into Reno, Nevada. They were crossing the Truckee River on the Virginia Street Bridge when confronted by Deputies Maxwell and Sharkey. The deputies fired their revolvers and Miller jumped in the river and escaped. Murphy was too slow on the draw and was handcuffed.

The next morning in Reno, Constable Wilson was standing on the corner of Center and Second Street. He saw Wood come around the corner and enter a barber shop. Wilson suspected who he was and, noticing that he was armed, went for backup. Returning with Chief Leeper, they drew their revolvers and went into the barber shop. Wood was being shaved and offered no resistance. The barber completed the shave. Wood talked freely saying he thought Wilson was a constable but thought it would be suspicious if he left the barber shop without a shave. He had arrived by train. He also knew he would be hanged. Both Wood and Murphy were heavily shackled and returned to Folsom. The rewards were paid in cash.

Other rewards were granted. Governor Pardee pardoned two convicts and commuted sentences of more. Joe Casey who aided Chalmers at the sally port was pardoned. Juan Martinez also helped Chalmers as did Ira Abbott. O. C. Clark, a nine-time convicted forger who kept the books in the captain's office, had run out giving the alarm and aided the wounded to the infirmary. William Grider was invaluable in aiding the wounded; he was also Harry Eldridge's cell partner and had informed Captain Murphy of the escape plot. The State Prison Commission met on November 21 to select Archibald Yell as the new warden, effective December 1. Both Charles Jolly and P. J. Cochrane recovered from their wounds and were promoted to lieutenant and captain respectively.

The first week in November, Fred Slocum was arrested in Yakima, Washington. He was thought to be escapee Theron. He claimed he had never been in prison but prison tattoos betrayed him. Under intense questioning he admitted that he had served time in Folsom. He gave his number as 4040 and had been discharged two weeks after the escape. He knew all of the escapees and was aware of the plot. Photos were taken of him and sent to Folsom for identification. Folsom officials verified that he was Slocum and had been discharged. So he was released to enjoy his first Thanksgiving dinner outside prison since 1897.

During the burglary of a hardware store in Trinidad, Colorado, Frank Miller was killed by the owner firing a shotgun. He was positively identified.

In early December, Wood was tried for the murder of guard Cotter in Sacramento County. Witnesses related that Wood and Murphy were the leaders. Wood was seen with a knife in the captain's office. During the trial bailiffs became worried because about twenty rough-looking men attended the trial. They were thought to be ex-convicts and they might aid Wood in escaping. Then a blackjack (a soft leather pouch usually filled with powdered lead, about ten inches long—in hand-to-hand fighting it is a deadly weapon) was found by a column only a few feet from Wood's route to and from the courtroom. Extra deputies were hired to maintain security.

In 1903, any convict serving a life sentence and convicted of assaulting any other person with malice and aforethought, using a weapon likely to cause bodily harm, was punishable by death. On December 9, 1903, at 10:15 A.M. the jury returned its verdict. The jury had deliberated all night. One juror had voted for acquittal twice, six times for murder first, then back to acquittal. Three had voted acquittal for twenty hours. They compromised with guilty of murder second.

Judge Hart was sarcastic in remarking, "Are you sure it isn't disturbing the peace?" The jury was polled and excused. Judge Hart ordered Wood to return in exactly one hundred years for sentencing. The sheriff opined that he might not be reelected to carry out the order but would pass the word onto his successors and their successors.

El Dorado County then indicted Wood for the murder of the two national guardsmen. His attorney tried several legal maneuvers and requested a change of venue. That failing, the trial started in March of 1904. Wood was identified as involved in the gunfight. His defense was in vain. Thirteen hours of deliberation resulted in a guilty verdict of murder one. The usual requests for a new trial were denied, so an appeal was filed. He was sentenced to be hanged.

Joe Murphy was tried next in Judge Hart's court. He was tried for Cotter's murder and testified cautiously. He was credible, but the verdict was murder one. The defense in asking for leniency said Murphy had served as a soldier in the Philippines. Apparently, after being discharged in San Francisco, he was robbed of his mustering-out pay, some $260. He became vengeful and became a footpad (mugger is the modern term). He did admit that he had always been bad.

R. W. Gordon was arrested in Jacksonville, Texas, by a city marshall. Extradition papers were signed and $550 paid and Gordon was returned to Folsom.

Funeral expenses in the amount of $291 were submitted for William Cotter to the prison accountant. The Prison Board thought $235 was adequate and refused to pay more. They refused to pay the medical bills of Cotter, Jolly and Cochrane because Jolly had requested a doctor. They ruled that a prison official must request a doctor in order for the state to pay. Cochrane couldn't request a doctor because he was unconscious at the time.

Harry Eldridge really had the most interesting time of all. Separating after the Pilot Hill gunfight, he traveled to Wadsworth, Nevada. He rejoined Miller there and together they went to Ogden, Utah. There he was arrested on misdemeanor charges and was shown pictures of the wanted escapees including himself. Asked if he had seen any of them he remarked he might have seen Miller "the Little Dutchman." However, Miller had been killed by this time.

He was released and he met an old acquaintance from Oakland, California, an ex-con. Eldridge won $250 in a card game so the pair went to Kansas City. Then they decided to go to British Columbia and work in the salmon canneries. Eldridge gave his friend $100 but the fellow got drunk and spent it all. Arriving in Seattle, Eldridge shared his last $20 with his friend and left for a saloon. The friend went straight to the King County Sheriff's Office. He tried to turn in Eldridge for the reward, but the older detectives ignored his pleas. Finally he interested Deputy J. Downey, the sheriff's nephew. Downey had just arrived from the east and was very new on the job. Eldridge was in a red light district saloon. The friend pointed him out to Downey and Eldridge was arrested. Eldridge denied his identity giving his name as Raymond. His many tattoos betrayed him when compared to the reward poster. Captain Cochrane arrived in Seattle on March 28 and left for Folsom the next day with Eldridge.

The prosecution presented a strong case. The jury was out two hours returning a murder-first verdict. Judge Gaddis pronounced sentence and Eldridge took it with no emotion. Back in jail he spoke to "Smiley" James Roberts saying he got the rope. Then they discussed the latest gossip about William Grider.

When Grider was released, he immediately secured employment at Weinstock and Lubin and Company. His employers soon learned of his criminal past and when confronted he pleaded so convincingly that the company resolved to help him mend his evil ways. Sheriff Reese was not so easily swayed by a smooth-talking sympathy seeker. The sheriff became convinced that Grider was implicated in a local robbery. In the meantime it was discovered that Grider had stored a lot of stolen goods in a basement at 1010 Third Street. He was also shipping goods to a Mrs. C. E. Pike in Fresno. The sheriffs and Weinstocks shared information and the sheriff of Fresno returned the goods. Grider was arrested and the stolen goods inventoried. There wasn't anything that he would not steal. Stoves, ribbons, lampshades, handkerchiefs, sofa pillows, buttons—the list was endless. Grider denied charges to deaf ears. On March 25, 1904, Grider wrote two sui-

91

cide notes. He tore his blankets into strips and braided a rope. He tied his feet together and stood on his slop bucket and secured the noose around his neck. He tied his hands together and slipped off the slop bucket. The rope broke. He served another term in Folsom.

Soon after his sentence was commuted, Ira Abbott operated a shoe shine stand in downtown Sacramento. After being wounded by Prigmore in 1893 he became a model prisoner and was very helpful in foiling the 1903 escape. Sheriff Reese received information that Abbott was involved in some local robberies. Abbott left town hurriedly for Chicago. There he received a life sentence in Joliet, Illinois, for robberies.

Roberts was next to be tried before Judge Hart in Sacramento. Roberts had been the dynamite man prepared to blow open the armory door. Since the warden's orders made explosions unnecessary, he was found guilty of murder two. So the judge gave him forty-five more years. Roberts made an eloquent plea for leniency so that he might die a free man. Judge Hart ordered the sentences to run concurrently.

Seavus was found guilty of murder second and returned to Folsom. The state paid the cost of his trial $180.35.

May 18, 1904, is a day that the Folsom staff would like to forget. Convict Charles Murray was twenty-one and serving ten years for grand larceny. He was working in the rock crusher gang. Over a period of time he had acquired and secreted a dark suit, white shirt, vest, tie and bowler hat in the quarry. He hid and dressed in his contraband clothing. About 10:30 A.M. he displayed a yardstick and monkey wrench. He tightened nuts on power poles then measured them several ways and noting the figures on his notepad. He paused to chat with staff and guards who assumed that he worked for the power company. Guards had been cautioned not to hinder the electric company workers. Eventually he wandered away. He took the train to San Francisco. There he stole the same horse from the same man who had him arrested and sent to prison. The same policeman arrested him again and back to the same Folsom Prison. This story demonstrates that the replacements of the fired guards were of lesser quality than those replaced.

After seventeen months District Attorney Seymour decided that he did not have sufficient evidence to convict Myers and Leverone. The charges were dropped. Myers and Leverone had been a vital part of the escape plot. They had attacked turnkey Chalmers at the outer sally gate with knives. One witness said Myers had cut Chalmers and killed William Cotter.

John Wood spent his time thinking about how he got where he was. About 11:30 P.M. of December 8, 1901, he was loitering on the corner of Pine and Sansome streets in San Francisco. Phillip Krell, a local citizen, had just finished eating a late dinner and was walking home. Woods pointed a revolver at Krell demanding his valuables. Wood reached for Krell's watch but Krell grabbed his hand and they struggled. Krell yelled for help and Policemen Leonard and Farrell ran to Krell's aid. Wood was overpowered and arrested. He gave his name as Frank Graham, recently from Arkansas and twenty-four years old. Later he admitted his name was John H. Wood. He was held in city jail till January 25, 1902.

That day Judge Cook sentenced him to life in Folsom saying, "something must be done to check the inclination of the semi-vagabond element in the city to turn footpads when pressed by wants often brought on by vicious living. The best remedy for this evil is long sentences."

"That's a pretty tough deal," said Wood seemingly unconcerned. The same day in Judge Dunne's courtroom, fellow escapee Edward Davis was sentenced to twenty-seven years for a similar crime.

Harris J. Wood was probably his real name and he was in the Forty-seventh Regiment of U.S. Volunteers. On September 30, 1899, he told the recruiter that he was twenty-two and had been born in Sulphur Springs, Hopson County, Texas. He enlisted in Memphis and was shipped to Camp Meade, Pennsylvania, and assigned to H Company. The regiment sailed from New York on November 4, 1899. On November 20, Wood tried to desert by sliding down a rope on the starboard side of the transport

Thomas. This could have been at Gibraltar or Port Said, Egypt. He was court-martialed and fined $10.

Wood never adjusted to military life and was the poorest example of what a soldier should be. He was twice court-martialed for being drunk and disorderly, once for hitting a Philippine citizen. He was tried for the robbery of a Philippine druggist, but was acquitted. He reported to the hospital with gonorrhea and chancroids. After treatment, he failed to return to his unit promptly. He failed to do his duty while guarding prisoners. Court-martialed for neglect, he was fined a month's pay and served thirty days at hard labor in the guardhouse. He was again court-martialed for being drunk and scuffling in a Chinese restaurant. Finally he deserted, but he was caught and court-martialed. He was sentenced to death by firing squad. His papers were sent to the War Department for approval of the sentence. Meanwhile he was returned to the U.S. on board the *Thomas* with the 47th Regiment. They arrived in San Francisco on June 26, 1901. The regiment of thirty-three officers and 971 enlisted were discharged at the Presidio. Wood was escorted to Alcatraz and confined.

The War Department disapproved the death sentence. A board of officers was convened at Alcatraz. They were to examine all general prisoners and submit recommendations looking to the release of such prisoners who deserved clemency. Emphasis was to center on conduct since confinement and men convicted of purely military offenses.

Wood was discharged dishonorably on July 1, 1901. His activities in the Bay area cannot be documented till his arrest in December. (Wood just couldn't follow the rules so he braided a rope from torn bed ticking and hanged himself in his cell on January 30, 1905.)

Joe Murphy was next. During June of 1905 he joked about being a short termer. He often sang and laughed. Walking out on the hangman's scaffold, he coolly looked around and without a word dropped into eternity on July 14.

December 1st of 1905 was the last for Harry Eldridge. He declined the consoling words of a man of God saying he just did not believe. He insisted that the warden read the death warrant. Eldridge approved the reading by the warden and, acting as if he didn't care, Eldridge stepped into the unknown.

Eight years after the initial escape, on a Monday morning in September of 1911, part of the finale was at hand. In the high prairies where North Dakota and Manitoba meet, school teacher Eleanor Gladys Price walked to school. Only one student attended that day so he was sent home with homework. About 11 A.M. while she was writing a letter, a man with a shotgun attacked her. She fought fiercely but was overpowered and carried into the woods. Concerned citizens found the signs of the struggle. Posses were formed and sent out.

About midnight Wednesday, Bill Adams, proprietor of the Weston House in Snowflake picked up his revolver and went downstairs to investigate noises. A man had eaten and was breaking into the bar. Several shots were exchanged in the dark and the intruder got away.

On Saturday morning citizens of Hannah, North Dakota, were notified by telephone that Ed Davis was at the Hallisey farm three miles east. Constables James Gleason and a hastily formed posse raced to the farm. Ed Davis was found in the hayloft and arrested. They were back in Hannah in thirty minutes.

Held at the State Bank, the prisoner gave his name and aliases. He readily confessed that he had escaped from Folsom in 1903. He said it took him seven months to reach Buenos Aires, Argentina, where he lived till three years earlier. Returning to the U.S., he worked on farms and burglarized stores. He would not fight extradition to California but he would fight returning to Manitoba. The locals then openly discussed lynching. Davis found some strychnine and took a large dose. The doctor pumped his stomach and he survived. He was extradited to Manitoba and spent the remainder of his life behind bars. Miss Price survived her attack.

There are far too many wrongs in this story. It was wrong for John Wood to desert after swearing allegiance to the U.S. Army. It was wrong for a judge to sentence Wood to life in Folsom for an attempted mugging. It was wrong for the governor of

California to appoint Thomas Wilkinson warden of Folsom Prison in return for political patronage. It was wrong for Warden Wilkinson to commit nepotism by hiring his nephew as a clerk. Wilkinson was wrong to accept the counsel of convict Raymond who forged the letter that caused Guard Prigmore to be fired. It was wrong for the other first-rate guards to be fired due to convict Raymond's influence. The state legislature abused its power in not paying its rightful bills caused by the escape. Deputy Sheriff Hinton acted properly and collected a reward. He could not legally accept a reward because he was a deputy sheriff. It seems that previously the sheriff fired Hinton so the sheriff could hire his own son as bailiff. The sheriff then fed his prisoners cheaper and shorter rations and paid Hinton's salary from the food budget. Some posse members were wrong and acted recklessly killing two innocent men. The judge was wrong when he disagreed with Wood's second-degree-murder conviction and ordered him to appear in exactly 100 years for sentencing.

Many fine lawmen acted properly in apprehending the escapees. They were about the only ones who were right.

References

San Francisco Call, San Francisco, CA
San Francisco Examiner, San Francisco, CA
Sacramento Bee, Sacramento, CA
Sacramento Union, Sacramento, CA
Placerville Nugget, Placerville, CA
Seattle Post-Intelligencer, Seattle, WA
Yakima Daily Republic, Yakima, WA
The Hannah Moon, Cavalier County, ND

Canadian Connection

In the first decade of this century, train robberies became popular. Banks would send large sums of cash to other banks by registered mail. Companies like Tiffany or Cartier would ship expensive jewelry to other companies by registered mail. The U.S. mint would print bank notes for local banks and ship by registered mail. Gold and silver were shipped by registered mail to the mint from western mines. The mail was insured and the mail clerks were armed. Railroad detectives were kept busy chasing bandits.

Hard men often dreamed of instant wealth and sometimes they carried out their dreams by robbing trains. Sometimes their luck was good and sometimes it was bad. Sometimes they were killed. Sometimes they looked over their shoulders for decades.

The evening of May 22, 1909, was developing into an enjoyable spring night in Omaha, Nebraska. Engineer A. R. Meiklejohn was operating the locomotive of the Union Pacific Overland Limited Number Two. The train left the station on time and was picking up speed to twenty miles per hour as it moved through South Omaha. At the bridge just east of Seymour, Meiklejohn noticed two men come over the water tank and both pointed automatic pistols at his face. It was 11:15 P.M. and Meiklejohn, fireman Roy Pratt and engineer Dave Wright were ordered to stop the train at a light near the entrance of Mud Cut or be shot. Not being fools, the train was stopped at the light. Meiklejohn was told not to coal the fire and to turn off the water. Then all five proceeded to the mail car.

There were nine mail clerks in the mail car. The door was slightly open but when the bandits and train crew arrived it was slammed shut by a clerk. The bandits pointed their weapons at the closed door and fired some shots demanding that the door be opened. The clerks opened the door and they were ordered out and lined up parallel to the train. One was ordered back into the

Scene of mail car robbery on Union Pacific Railroad near Omaha, May 22, 1909.

Photo: Union Pacific Museum Collection

mail car accompanied by one bandit and they threw out registered mail sacks. Another bandit threatened to kill the clerks if the bandit in the mail car was harmed in any way. Occasionally shots were fired into the ground or air to emphasize an order. Nine sacks of registered mail were thrown on the ground. The bandits ordered the clerks to carry them up the track to a previously selected spot. The clerks were then ordered to return to the train, which they were relieved to do. It took the train crew some time to coal the fire and build up steam. After arriving at the next station the crew notified the Omaha police and railroad management. The bandits had taken the mail sacks and disappeared.

The train crew reported that at least four and maybe five bandits were involved. They had worn long rain coats, slouch hats and blue polka dot handkerchiefs as masks. Descriptions were of little use, but two were heavy set and in their thirties and one was about twenty. Meiklejohn and Pratt thought they might identify two by their voices. Clerk Whitmore thought he might recognize one.

The Omaha police detectives along with railroad detectives investigated. Speculation was that the gang had robbed a train near Spokane, Washington, only two weeks previous. A bunco scheme and a street car robbery were blamed on them.

How true it is that it is better to be lucky than good. Six days after the robbery, John Vavra, the janitor at Brown Park School noticed that a rope was off of the pulley that lowered the attic ladder. The attic was used for storage of some lumber scraps. Vavra thought some school boys had been playing up there and he investigated. He found cut open mail sacks and pieces of mail all over the floor. He notified the police.

Close by the school house were a slough and a gully which led into the slough. Young school boys sometimes played in the gully for reasons known only to young, inquisitive minds. John Krolik, a student, had a habit of rolling down the gully on his way home from the school. Thursday afternoon of the 27th he saw the tip of a leather belt sticking up from the soil. Stanley Perina, his friend, helped him pull the belt out of the soil. It was a gun belt with an automatic pistol in a holster. Little Johnnie ran home and showed the pistol to his grandmother. Seeing it she cried, "No, don't touch it. It may be set to kill us." Johnnie went back to the cache and recovered more pistols, bullets, overalls, a hat and polka dot handkerchiefs. Other children grouped around and Principal Margaret Hays called the Omaha police to investigate the cache. Detectives, immediately suspecting the nature of the cache, seized the evidence and told the boys to keep a lookout on the site. They were to report any suspicious characters who might appear to claim the cache.

It was the most thrilling night of the boys' lives. They were wide awake and alert when four men slowly approached the cache then left quickly to enter a saloon. They separated only to reappear at the cache. Omaha detectives Mawhinney and Turnquist were summoned. They arrested three men, the fourth slipped away. The three gave their names as Woods, Torgeson and Gordon. All were aliases so to simplify identification they were Dan Downer, Fred Derf and Frank Grigware. They were booked into jail and questioned and questioned. All denied any

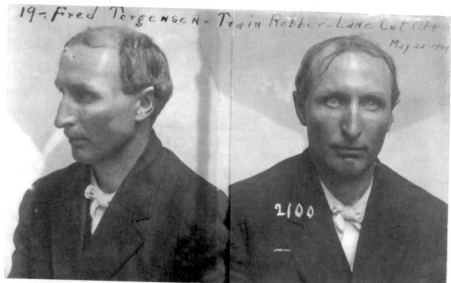

Fred Torgensen, May 22, 1909.

Photo: Union Pacific Museum Collection

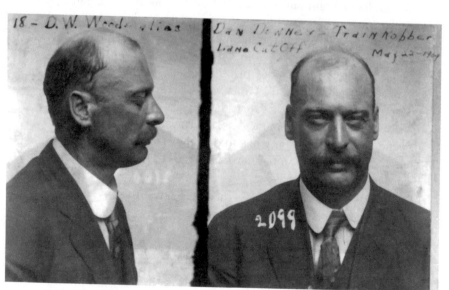

D. W. Woods, May 22, 1909.

Photo: Union Pacific Museum Collection

Picture Traced By Alert Newshawk Brings Conviction Grigware As Omaha Mail Bandit

Reporter's Ingenuity Enabled Police to Follow Men's Movements

TAKEN IN DENVER

A vigilant and enterprising newspaper reporter played an important part in the trial that resulted in the conviction of James Fahey (Frank Grigware) and four other men on a charge on robbing a mail train at Omaha, it is revealed in a story from the Edmonton Journal's correspondent at Omaha, Nebraska. A picture was found in a room occupied by some of the alleged robbers. The reporter discovered where the picture had been taken and who the men where and this knowledge led to the arrest of five men.

One Copy Forgotten

This picture was made in Denver, Colorado. Following the arrest of three members of the bandit crew, two others were sought. One of these made his way, secretly, to Denver and destroyed all the copies of this picture that were known by him to exist. But he forgot the copy which Grigware had brought to Omaha with him. He also destroyed all the letters which the girl in the picture had received from members of the gang.

Woods, the man at the wheel, was the first robber captured. After the holdup the robbers buried their pistols under a rubbish heap near Brown Park school. Some little boys, playing around the rubbish, discovered the pistols. The police were notified. A trap was set and when Woods came for his gun, he was arrested.

Half an hour later Frank Grigware and Fred Torgensen were arrested close to the rubbish heap. They denied any participation in, or knowledge of the robbery. They refused to recognize Woods when taken to the jail where the latter was a prisoner.

A fourth man was seen near the rubbish heap but escaped by leaping down a high dirt embankment. At that time there was nothing connecting Grigware and Torgensen with the crime. They denied knowing anything about the buried pistols.

Then a newspaper reporter found this picture in a rooming house at 15th and Davenport streets in Omaha. First, he located the house in which the suspects had boarded. This old picture was in the room. It showed that Grigware was on friendly terms with the two men who were under arrest. And in the pockets of the latter two were

(Continued on Page 6, Col. 2)

This is the picture that led to the arrest of James Fahey and members of a gang who were convicted of robbing a mail train and sentenced to life imprisonment, Fahey escaping in 1910 and fleeing to Canada. The picture was taken some time before the robbery in a studio at Denver, and was used in the trial to establish the friendship of the four men. At the wheel of the "fake" automobile is D. W. Woods, leader of the gang, and besides him, Lillian Stevenson, associate of Woods, who testified in the trial that Golden, alias Jack Gordon had tried to destroy all copies of the photo. The other man in the front row is Fred Torgenson. Behind Woods is Grigware (Fahey) and behind Torgenson is Golden. Woods was arrested first.

wrong doing. They were just ordinary working men from Spokane, Washington.

The expended cartridge cases found at the robbery scene matched the calibers of the weapons found at the cache. One automatic when fired dented the cartridge case in a peculiar way. An automatic found at the cache produced a similar marking. Thus it was determined that the weapon was used in the holdup. At the time, ballistic science was in its infancy.

Derf and Grigware denied that they knew Downer but police found a photograph that disclaimed that. The photo was taken in a Denver studio in a fake automobile. Downer, Derf, Grigware, Shelton and a Miss Lillian Stevenson were all smiling in the photo.

Jack Shelton and Miss Stevenson were arrested on June 2 in a Curtis Street rooming house by Denver detectives. They were brought to Omaha for questioning. Miss Stevenson acknowledged that she and Shelton had been lovers for about six weeks. She also agreed to testify in court and disclose all that she knew.

The Grand Jury indicted all four but the police kept looking for the fifth accomplice. William Matthews was arrested in Buhl, Idaho. Pinkerton detectives had suspected him because he was a known acquaintance of the four accused. He was brought to Omaha and a rooming-house landlady positively identified him as a man who had visited Jack Shelton, a tenant of her establishment.

The five languished in jail refusing to turn state's evidence. They obtained attorneys and prepared their defense. The detectives continued to question witnesses and collect evidence.

On October 25, 1909, at 2 P.M. Judge Thomas C. Munger started the trial. More than 100 witnesses were scheduled to testify. Fifty-two jury men were called and twelve were selected by the October 27. Engineer Meiklejohn was called first and positively identified Downer and Derf as the two gunmen who accosted him in the locomotive cab. Other witnesses verified the identification. Frederick Eastman, one of the postal clerks, identified Downer and Derf positively and was certain that Grigware was another bandit. Several of the school boys testified and identified all but Matthews. Principal Margaret Hayes testified that she saw Matthews and the others carefully examining the school and surrounding area. Upon cross-examination she proved to be a very credible witness. A tailor from Kansas City testified that he made a suit for Matthews, and Grigware was with Matthews at the fittings. This suit was found in Matthews' possession with a Kansas City label intact.

Edward Hoffman, a detective from Colorado Springs, Colorado, testified that he knew Grigware as E. E. Hollingsworth. James Schroeder of Spokane testified that he had sold Grigware a .38-caliber Colt revolver in 1908; he also played on the same baseball team. Lillian Stevenson, a reluctant witness, testified carefully so as to protect her lover and thus neither helped nor hurt the prosecution's case.

The trial attorneys continued to work hard and so did the bandits. For several nights the sound of sawing could be faintly heard in the jail. Finally jailers found the source of the noise. In Dan Downer's cell were two hacksaw blades and twenty-five feet of rope and a hole cut in the cell ceiling. Three three-foot-long gas pipes were found in the hole. Derf and Grigware, who shared a cell had six hacksaw blades. A young woman, under the guise of being a religious worker, had been calling at the jail. The saws were found in a basket of fruit she had given to the prisoners. An extra jailer was added to the night watch with orders to carefully watch the five.

The defense was brief. Frank Grigware's father told of his son's good character and that he believed him innocent. The jury was given the case at 4:50 P.M. on November 11; two hours and twenty minutes later they returned with a guilty verdict. A defense attorney gave notice of appeal. Judge Munger told him to file it by 9 A.M. the next day.

Apparently there was some doubt whether William Matthews might be found guilty. In case he was found innocent, Sheriff Felix M. Pugh of Spokane was in the courtroom with a fugitive warrant for Matthews. It charged he was a fugitive from justice having forfeited a $5,000 bail for cattle rustling. The sheriff elaborated to the press that, "Matthews and I are old acquaintances. We had a little shooting scrape nineteen years ago in Washington.

I was after him and his pal John Miles and cornered them. The shooting started and I shot Matthews twice in the arm and he got me once in the leg. Miles was killed and Matthews got away. Matthews is a bad man through and through."

Attorney arguments delayed the appeal for a few days. On Thursday, the eighteenth, Judge Munger denied a new trial. He then sentenced all five to the federal prison at Leavenworth, Kansas, for the remainder of their natural lives. All but Downer proclaimed their innocence, but their pleas fell on deaf ears.

It was never determined just how much money and valuables was stolen. When captured the bandits had very little money on their persons.

Rewards totaling almost $30,000 had been offered for the arrest and conviction of the train robbers. Attorneys for the young boys sued to claim it. After a long, bitter legal battle John Krolik, John Swoboda, Harry Whitaker, John Polach and Anton Kubat, ages eight to twelve, each received $2,000 minus legal fees.

The convicted bandits arrived at Leavenworth on November 19, 1909. Grigware soon had a prison nickname of "Frigidaire." Either it was a corruption of Frank Grigware or he was one cool dude. Since he was a shingler and a carpenter, as was his father, he was assigned to work in the carpenter shop.

Five months passed. On April 21, 1910, at 8:30 A.M. the convicts were starting the work day when a locomotive and flatcar backed into the prison yard. Four convicts from the carpenter shop and two from the tailor shop ran to the train and boarded it. They were armed with wooden guns that looked real. They told the engineer to give the signal to open the railroad gates. He did and simultaneously opened the throttle. The inner gate of the sally port was open but the outer gate was closed. It was made of heavy steel bars. The locomotive hit it at about ten miles per hour reducing it to scrap instantly. The throttle was kept open as the engine raced through the hills and neared Shanghai Bridge in Salt Creek Valley. Engineer Charles Curtain told the escapees that a pile driver was working there and to maintain speed through there would mean certain death for all. He was allowed to slow the engine and they saw that he was truthful. Curtain stopped at the bridge and the desperadoes all jumped to the ground. Curtain was told to draw the coals of the fire so as not to have enough steam to move for some time. Curtain was relieved of his coat and cap and dinner pail. They also took the shirt and coat from the fireman. They all disappeared into the woods. After getting up steam Curtain returned to the prison to ferry guards back to the bridge to begin searching for the escapees.

Local farmers hearing the escape whistle quickly armed themselves. They all knew the sound and capturing a convict was worth a $50 reward. Farmer Fred Frey and his seventeen-year-old son soon saw three escapees and shouted for them to halt. Two

UNITED STATES · PENITENTIARY · LEAVENWORTH KANSAS.

$100 REWARD

Classification

FRANK GRIGWARE, No. 6768 (aliases James Gordon, E. grigwald). Escaped from the United States Penitentiary, at Leavenworth, Kansas. April 21, 1910.

Ref.

ESCAPE $100. REWARD — IF APPREHENDED, WIRE T. B. WHITE, Acting Warden

DESCRIPTION: White, age 23 (in 1909), height 5 feet 8½ inches in bare feet, weight 161 pounds, fair complexion, light brown hair, blue eyes, light brown beard. Scar ¼ inch oblique inner at 3d phalanx left at 3d finger front. Small scar of ¼ inch vertical at 2d phalanx right thumb rear. Pit scar at ¼ inch below right eye; 2d and 3d toes of each foot web.

Received November 19, 1909, from Omaha, Nebraska, under sentence of life for robbing U. S. mail train. Occupation, carpenter. Residence, Spokane, Washington.

Bertillon Measurements: 174.8, 182.0, 93.5, 19.7, 16.4, 14.0, 6.4, 25.7, 11.5, 9.3, 47.8.

Finger Print Classification: $\frac{25 \quad IO \quad 14}{9 \quad OO \quad 17}$

CIRCULAR ISSUED JAN. 1927

$100 REWARD $100

FRANK GRIGWARE, No. 6768

Aliases James Gordon, E. E. Hollingshead

Escaped from the United States Penitentiary, Leavenworth, Kansas, April 21, 1910.

DESCRIPTION: White, age 23 (in 1909), height 5 feet 8½ inches in bare feet, weight 161 pounds, fair complexion, light brown hair, blue eyes, light brown beard. Scar ½ inch oblique inner at 3d phalanx left 3d finger front. Small scar of ½ inch vertical at 2d phalanx right thumb rear. Pit scar at ½ inch below right eye; 2d and 3d toes of each foot web.

RECEIVED November 19, 1909, from Omaha, Nebraska, under sentence of life for robbing U. S. mail train. Occupation, carpenter. Residence, Spokane, Washington.

BERTILLON	174.8, 182.0, 93.5, 19.7, 16.4, 14.0, 6.4, 25.7, 11.5, 9.3, 47.8.
Finger print classification:	25 10 14 / 9 00

$100.00 Reward will be paid for his delivery, after identification has been made, to an authorized officer of this Penitentiary.

Arrest and wire:
A. V. ANDERSON, Warden

ran but Bob Clark surrendered when he saw Frey's shotgun pointed at him. Frey and son marched Clark back to the prison and then told him that the shotgun wasn't loaded. John Gideon was captured next by guards. Then Hewitt and Kating were captured at 2 P.M. by guards near Lund School House. Theodore Murdock was captured the next day. His first words to the capturing guards were, "Get me back to the prison so I can get something to eat." Frank Grigware was the only one to elude the searchers. Three thousand circulars were distributed with Grigware's description offering a reward dead or alive. He was twenty-four years old, 5'8 1/2", 165 pounds, fair complexion and the second and third toes of his feet were webbed.

An investigation disclosed that Hewitt and Kating planned the escape. They had also planned the mass escape in 1901 when twenty-nine convicts broke out of Leavenworth. The dummy revolvers used were almost exact copies of Colt revolvers. They were made of wood in the carpenter shop. The barrels were painted steel color. The walnut grips looked authentic. Brass cartridge cases and lead bullets were meticulously crafted. It took a very close examination to reveal they were fakes.

Memories fade with the passage of time. Prison boards become lenient and reduce sentences. Jack Shelton was pardoned on August 12, 1913. Dan Downer and Fred Derf were pardoned on July 7, 1919. William Matthews was discharged on July 7, 1920. Perhaps that shootout with the sheriff cost him an extra year.

On March 10, 1934, James Fahey was arrested for poaching martens in Jasper National Park by Royal Canadian Mounted Police. He was booked, photographed and fingerprinted according to custom. He pled guilty to poaching and was fined $200. The records were filed and in due course replies from Ottawa revealed that James Fahey was Frank Grigware, train robber and prison escapee. Fahey was rearrested in his home in Jasper on a fugitive warrant. He did not deny his true identity, just sat stunned and quietly thinking. He was moved to Calgary for confinement pending extradition proceedings to the United States.

Local Canadians were stunned and confused in disbelief. Fahey had a wife and three children and was very active in

Case Becomes International Affair
Appeals for Aid Flood White House
Ex-Companion 'Lifer' Urges Merc

FIRST PICTURES OF FAHEY CHILDREN

Ex-Fugitive Faintly
calls Acquaintance of
Former Years

SILENT ON HOLDUP

Convicted With Grigwa
Man Served Seven
Years of Term

Waiting in Jasper for the final freedom of their beloved father, out on bail pending efforts of the United States government to extradite him as an escaped lifer from Leavenworth penitentiary, the three children of James Fahey and Mrs. Fahey are being cared for by friends in their beautiful mountain home. These are the first pictures to be published of the three children and were obtained exclusively by the Journal. (1) Is Louise Fahey, 13, with the dog that is favorite of the household, (2) Is Jack Fahey, 15, born when the Fahey family was homesteading near Spirit River, and (3) is Marie Fahey, eight, born after the

Case of James Fah
Jasper resident held on b
as Frank Grigware, fu
tive from Leavenwo
penitentiary. Wednesc
assumed proportions of
delicate international m
ter. Officials in Washi
ton and Ottawa declin
comment, but it was hin
in high circles that eith
a presidential pardon f
the man might be issued
else the United States
partment of justice mig
drop the extradition p
ceedings it has institut
against Fahey. In any ca
developments are expect
almost within a few hou
The White House We
nesday was feeling
ever-growing flood of w
ten and telegraphed a

(Continued from Page 9, Col.

Fahey Fails

Hope For Re-uniting Jasper Family Grows, Two Premiers Assisting; Companion 'Lifers' Already Free

HUSBAND AND WIFE RE-UNITED

Two Jasper Friends Post
$10,000 Bail in
Property Values

May 12, 1934.

The Honorable
The Secretary of State.

My dear Mr. Secretary.

In reply to your letter of May 2, 1934, relative to the proceeding for the extradition of Frank Grigware from Canada, I desire to say that after careful consideration of all the facts bearing on this matter I have reached the conclusion that the ends of justice would be best served by not insisting that Grigware be extradited.

I should, therefore, be glad if you would be good enough to withdraw the request for his extradition.

Sincerely yours,

Homer Cummings
Attorney General.

DIVISION OF INVESTIGATION

U. S. DEPARTMENT OF JUSTICE

WASHINGTON, D. C.

May 17, 1934

FINGERPRINT
CLASSIFICATION:

10 25 W IO 14
     9 U OO 17

APPREHENSION ORDER
No. 1148-304.

Dear Sir:

In Re: FRANK GRIGWARE, aliases,
JAMES GORDON, E. HOLLINGSHEAD.

Identification Order 1148 on the above named subject is hereby cancelled, inasmuch as he was taken into custody at Edmonton, Alberta, Canada on March 29, 1934.

Very truly yours,

J. E. Hoover,

Director.

church activities. He was a builder of fine homes in Jasper. Friends spoke of his sterling character and honesty. He was perhaps the most-respected man in Jasper. No one said a derogatory word in describing him or his family.

He told his life story to the press. He was born in Michigan in 1888 and his family moved to Spokane when he was twelve. He became a carpenter and shingler but drifted around. In Omaha he was arrested for robbing a train, for which he claimed innocence. While working in the carpenter shop in Leavenworth he took advantage of an escape plot. After leaving the train he quickly separated from the others and hid and walked for three days. He asked at a farm house for a meal to satisfy his hunger. The farmer's wife fed him and gave him a coat. He traveled north. He found work in Minnesota. He started using his mother's maiden name of Fahey. He worked in Duluth, Winnipeg, Port Arthur, Yorkton and Rainbow, Saskatchewan. Finally he homesteaded at Spirit River. He met Miss Ruth G. Brodrick, a pretty school teacher, and they married December 20, 1916. Three children were born to this union. In 1924 they sold the homestead for $3,000 and moved to Jasper. He built homes there.

Soon public opinion was overwhelmingly in favor of releasing Fahey. Petitions circulated requesting a pardon from President Roosevelt. Local civic leaders posted bail and Fahey was released from custody. The town of Jasper pledged the entire value of the town to aid in securing his permanent release.

U.S. Congressman Shoemaker from Minnesota lent his influence as did Premier Bennett. Even Judge Munger, Omaha's police chief in 1909 Henry W. Dunn, mail clerk Fred Eastman, federal prosecutor Charles Goss all recommended forgiveness. In fact, no one who spoke out advocated returning Fahey to Leavenworth. His wife Ruth stood by her man, her love or devotion never wavering in her belief in him. Surely she was one of God's finest creations.

Due to the amount of publicity it became known that Frank Grigware's parents and brother were alive and well. His mother said she had never given up hope that she would find her son alive and well someday. He had never written to them in twenty-four years for obvious reasons. On April 20, the family reunited in Jasper. A white-haired grandmother saw her son after twenty-four years and three grandchildren she didn't know she had a few weeks previously. United States Attorney General Homer Cummings dropped extradition proceedings.

Now that's better than a shootout for an ending don't you think?

References

Omaha Daily Bee, Omaha, NE
The Spokesman Review, Spokane, WA
Edmonton Journal, Edmonton, Alberta
Department of Justice, Bureau of Prisons, Washington, DC
Leavenworth Daily Times, Leavenworth, KS
Union Pacific Railroad Company, Omaha, NE

Puzzle of the Purcell Mountains

In the summer of 1910 the ghost town of Sylvanite was coming back to life. From 1897 to 1899 it had been a thriving metropolis of almost 600 people. As with most mining towns, the ores were not plentiful or rich enough to sustain a large population for very long. The miners and merchants moved on in hopes that the next camp would fulfill their dreams of wealth and leisure. Fritz Lang, stayed on as a watchman for the absentee owners of the Keystone Mine.

The Keystone Mine owners had interested some Canadian investors who began to hire mining engineers. The engineers had new ideas to try in smelting the ores. The Goldflint Mills and the Keystone Mine combined and thirty stamps were ready to crush the ores. (Stamps are large heavy weights that are dropped repeatedly on silver ore, thereby crushing it to almost a powder. Then the reduced ore is treated with various chemicals, such as cyanide, to separate the silver from its original form. Almost all ores at that time were crushed in stamp mills.) Twenty men were employed and more arrived daily. A sawmill was scheduled to open. Lots were selling to merchants. A telephone line was installed. The future looked bright for this little in the northwest corner of Montana a few miles from both Canada and Idaho.

Early on August 27, the dreaded fire alarm was sounded. Women and children were loaded in wagons and left for the safety of Troy, a settlement several miles to the south. The citizens tried to telephone Troy for men to help fight the fire. The line was dead. Stanley Wood was dispatched on a fast horse for help. He found the telephone wire cut. It was cut cleanly near an insulator and not an accidental break.

Eventually help arrived and the men fought the fire for three days. The firefighters fought the hardest to save Harry

Cobbledeck's Hotel and they were successful. It was the only building saved. The bar was well stocked until the firefighters wet their parched throats. Almost 100 homes and businesses were destroyed. The monetary loss was estimated at $70,000. The town and mines were burned from one mile north to three miles south. The town never recovered.

Eventually nature regenerated the area to a beautiful pristine wilderness. Tall evergreens and birch and aspen trees covered steep mountain slopes. The water in the streams ran crystal clear and full of shining trout. The woods were full of deer, bear and grouse. Who would burn down this Rocky Mountain wilderness and why?

Charles McDonald, the villain of this story, was an alcoholic and when drunk had a vicious temper. He also had a reason.

In the remote Rocky Mountain wilderness of northwestern Montana the Kootenai River flows south along the Purcell Mountains. Its water is swift and cold because it comes from melting snow. Perhaps it is somewhat comforting that the Great Northern Railroad accompanies it for many miles. On September 12, 1907, the Great Northern *Oriental Limited*, the most luxurious train in the Northwest, was westbound from Minneapolis/St. Paul to Seattle, Washington. It had a fifty-eight-hour schedule from Minneapolis/St. Paul to Seattle. The wind blew and it rained hard throughout the dark night. Engineer Silas Schutt looked at his watch noting it was 2:30 A.M. Fred Pierson had just finished shoveling coal into the firebox and it was warm and dry in the engine cab. As Pierson stood up, he turned around to see a revolver pointed at his head.

Two masked bandits had entered the cab and ordered the crew, "You are stuck up, do as I tell you and nobody will be hurt." Schutt and Pierson were searched for weapons by the bandits but they did not have any. Schutt was ordered to stop the train by a certain telegraph pole near a steep cliff. There the bandits' partner waited with a supply of weapons and ammunition and dynamite. The two bandits, forcing Schutt and Pierson to accompany them, went to the extra express car. There the bandits ordered the express clerks out of the car upon peril of their lives. They came out and were ordered to the rear of the train. The bandits and cab crew entered the express car and exploded a charge to open the safe. The charge failed to open the safe. A second charge was exploded and it too failed its purpose. The third blew the door open and destroyed the express car. The bandits then took mail pouches and anything else that looked valuable.

All this time the bandits' partner, who was located on the top of the steep cliff, fired his revolver parallel to the train cars to dissuade the brave or curious from approaching too close. The tallest bandit would move from side to side also firing his weapon parallel to the train. Conductor Hurley told a brakeman to run the six miles back to Rexford and telegraph for help. The shorter bandit carried two revolvers both tied to his coat sleeves by cords. He gave all the orders and once called a partner "Mac." The bandits frequently looked at their watches and after fifty minutes decided it was time to go.

They grabbed their loot and ran down to the river. There they had previously tied a raft; they boarded it and pushed out into the current. The raft was made of thirty-foot-long telegraph poles with five-foot boards nailed across the poles. The paddle and/or rudder was a five-foot board. The poor design and poorer construction combined with an inadequate guidance system caused the craft to founder on rocks less than a mile downstream from where they boarded. With the swiftness of the current combined with rain and darkness it is a small wonder that the occupants didn't drown. Their rifle and shotgun were lost but they held onto the loot and stumbled west.

A hobo named Umbray who had watched the robbery from start to finish walked up and down the train telling the crew and passengers it was all over. He had been riding the blind baggage and saw the bandits board at Rexford. He claimed he saw them clearly and could identify them positively. (Later when lawmen learned this they arrested him and held him as a material witness for months.) The train then resumed its journey and arrived in Spokane about 1 P.M. The roof and sides of car 577 were badly damaged from the dynamite charges. It was left on a siding for extensive repairs.

Conductor Hurley and other crewmen gave descriptions of the responsibles. One was 5'11", about 180 pounds, had slightly stooped shoulders, dark hair, was wearing a black sack coat and pants, a black slouch hat and appeared to be in his forties. The other was 5'6", 135 pounds, with a black sack coat and khaki pants, and in his thirties.

Flathead County sheriff William H. O'Connell and eight special deputies boarded a train in Kalispell, some 200 miles east of Spokane, just after daylight. Arriving at the scene at Rondo Siding they asked questions and searched for evidence. They found more than 150 expended cartridge cases, mostly .40-80 rifle, some 12-gauge shotgun and the rest .38 revolver. They found the bandits' old camp where the raft had been made. A partial box of dynamite and an ax that had been stolen from a small farm owned by Joe Murphy was found. The short bandit had been a regular customer of Fewkes Store at Rexford. J. C. Sullivan, a local man, said he had met three men on a raft and they offered to buy his boat, but he declined to sell.

The posse did not start the pursuit that day but waited till Harry Draper and his famous bloodhounds arrived the next day. Draper was famous all over the Pacific Northwest for having reliable dogs that usually found what they were looking for. The hounds took the scent but the trail led uphill over slick rocks, through brush and more rocks. It was too hard on the dogs to follow the trail. Their feet were cut, they were scratched by the brush and the posse was ready to try something else. The search was temporarily called off to rest the dogs.

On September 15 in Bonners Ferry, Idaho, James Sharkey was arrested on suspicion. He had been working as a compass man for the Bonners Ferry Lumber Company in Montana but was fired. He went to Bonners Ferry and started drinking and talking. He said that he knew when and where the *Oriental Limited* was going to be robbed before it was robbed. The sheriff held him hoping to gain more information, but eventually he was released.

That same day G. H. Boulton and his brother had been fishing at Fish Lake near the Canadian border of British Columbia and saw three men cooking a meal. The brothers noted the men

115

did not have any equipment and were afoot. They fit the description of the bandits. Chief Dow of Cranbrook, B.C., investigated but found nothing.

Pat McCue or McHugh was arrested in Spokane by Officer Lister on suspicion of being a low character. (At the time this occurred, it was common for lawmen to arrest men who loitered or traveled a lot, like hobos. They could be charged with vagrancy or just being a low character. Often they were sentenced to jail and put to work on public projects like road construction. Also a lawman would encounter a low character and escort him to the edge of town and tell him not to return or be jailed. Sometimes a lawman would invite a homeless drifter to spend the night in an empty jail cell and leave the next morning. They would be noted in the jail register as "lodger.") McCue was searched and Lister found two nickels that appeared to have been in an explosion. They were black and powder blown. He also had a ten-dollar gold certificate. He was strongly suspected of being implicated in burglarizing a tailor shop the previous spring. His companions were known safe-crackers. Further questioning proved fruitless and he was released at the edge of town and cautioned not to return.

The general manager of the Great Northern Railroad R. E. Ward offered a $5,000 reward for the arrest and conviction of the train robbers. Later in combination with the state of Montana and the Marine Insurance Company of London through their agents Chubb and Sons, the rewards totaled $15,410. An inventory disclosed that $40,000 had been stolen from the registered mail pouches en route from the Commercial Bank of Chicago to the Old National Bank of Spokane. Other packages were seized and it would have taken a lot of time to verify all the losses to determine the exact amount stolen.

The bandits moved west through the Purcell Mountains. It was very hard traveling. Brush was thick and the ground steep. It was wet and cold. There was frost every night at that elevation. They were reluctant to have a fire at night as they might be spotted. So they shivered and went hungry but they were immensely comforted knowing that what they carried was worth the suffering. They entered the ghost town of Sylvanite after dark and hid most of the loot in the Chickadee Mine, then slipped away. Seventeen days after the robbery, two of the bandits casually entered Leonia, a town south of Sylvanite, and boarded the eastbound train for Butte, Montana.

Disembarking at Butte, they went straight to the ABC Saloon on Wyoming Street near the corner of Mercury Street. It was the red-light and saloon district. They deposited $3,000 with Lucien Ravarat, the proprietor. They invited all present to join them in lifting a glass. A large, thirsty crowd soon was enjoying their largess. It was whiskey and women on their minds and a song on their lips. The short bandit renewed his relationship with a local prostitute, Pearl Raymond. She had a friend for his friend. They ate and drank and slept for several days. The bandits paid for everything.

The two bandits and their girlfriends decided to go to Salt Lake City. They boarded the train and ordered drinks. The taller bandit's girlfriend spoke to the conductor and the bandit became enraged. He threatened to kill the girl if she spoke to anyone else. They only stayed in Salt Lake two days. Returning to Butte and the ABC Saloon, the party continued. The group visited other saloons. Butte had more than 200 saloons and they never closed. Most didn't have locks on the doors. Those that were built with locks had a key ritual. During the grand opening ceremonies, the owner would throw the key in the toilet and many enjoyed several toasts.

During this ongoing party one evening a fireman named Casey from the Arizona Street Station met the foursome and a fight started. It seems that Casey thought the girl with the taller bandit was his true love and was jealous. The fight was quickly broken up but Casey swore out an arrest warrant and the bandit was arrested. Lucien Ravarat was summoned and posted bail of $50 for Charles E. McDonald's release. The party continued till the money started to run out. The bandits excused themselves saying they had to go to the coast, but first they had to stop in Bonners Ferry, Idaho, on a money matter.

The corner of Mercury and Wyoming Streets in Butte, Montana. This is one block north of where the ABC Saloon was located. It would have looked very similar. These buildings look sad now but a short century ago they were the mainstay of a lifestyle never again to be repeated.   *Photo: Norman Davis*

Riley's Dance Hall on Main Street, Bonners Ferry, Idaho. In more recent times the remodeled front didn't attract enough business so it closed. The sign boasts "Since 1895."   *Photo: Norman Davis*

Leaving the train in Bonners Ferry, they introduced themselves as mining men. They rented a fine team of horses and a
luxurious buggy from Elderton's Livery and Feed Stable. The
pair drove east and north about thirty-five miles to Sylvanite.
Fritz Lang, the town's sole occupant, was lonely and he invited
the wayfarers to spend the night. Lang was eager for news of the
outside world and he prepared a fine breakfast to show his appre-
ciation for the latest news. The pair then walked to the Chickadee
Mine and returned about 10:30 A.M. and immediately left for
Bonners Ferry. They told Fritz they would return and stay longer
but the horses required fodder. Returning to Bonners Ferry they
stopped at the Cooper Ranch and Mrs. Cooper sold them a lard
pail and a stone crock with a lid for five dollars. They told her
they needed the containers to hold ore samples. They spent the
night with E. W. Newton and were back in Bonners Ferry the
next day. They decided to have a drink.

They checked into the Casey Hotel and went to Riley's
Dance Hall that evening. They must have had hangovers, as they

had a quiet evening spending about $30 each. The next morning
they stood around Riley's Dance Hall in their underwear while
their clothing was being cleaned. They had a gray overcoat that
they never let out of their sight. They intended to buy a new
wardrobe in Spokane. They invited Tom Riley, the congenial
dance hall host, to accompany them to the coast and he agreed.
That night McDonald got drunk, but his partner stayed sober.
They called for alcohol just to break bottles. They would order
drinks for everyone, break the bottles, buy more rounds, tip the
prostitutes, break bottles and buy rounds. They asked to lock the
doors with only the girls and bartenders present and broke every
bottle in the saloon. McDonald tried to buy the mirror just so he
could break it but Riley talked him out of it. Then he wanted to
break up the bar. He went looking for an ax but returned without
one, and since the bar was dry they went to the Olympic and
drank it dry. Then the Cariboo and every saloon in town till there
was not a bottle left in town. A telegram was sent to Sand Point
urging the good people there to send liquor immediately. A
wagon was dispatched for potent potables promptly. This was

when a miner earned $4 a day and the revelers spent about $500 in six hours. They bought the girls $40 kimonos.

Jesse Howe put his suspicions to Thomas Riley and they agreed that the pair must be the train robbers. The smaller one fit the description but the taller one didn't exactly match, but they were willing to overlook that. Riley introduced Howe to the pair and invited Howe to accompany them to the coast. Riley and Howe sent a telegram to detectives in Spokane outlining their suspicions and detective Aleck MacDonald organized an arrest team to meet the train. The four left Bonners Ferry on Friday morning and ordered beer and whiskey immediately upon entering the drawing room. They had to buy whiskey in one-drink bottles so they bought a dozen and tipped generously. They played cards, smoked and drank till McDonald got the urge to break out the train windows. He claimed he had done it before and was determined to do it again. The three finally talked him out of it.

The arrest team boarded the train at Hillyard just north of Spokane. As the train slowed entering the city limits of Spokane railroad detective Aleck MacDonald and three others burst into the drawing room shouting "Throw up your hands, all of you; I'll kill the first man who goes for his pocket." All four raised their hands and were handcuffed. At the terminal the party took buggies to the city jail. The bandits were separated from Riley and Howe and charged as fugitives. Jailer Wallace and Sergeant McPhee searched the bandits' clothing. The onlookers were stupefied as package after package of money was found. The total was $14,100. None present had ever seen that much money. There was no other incriminating evidence found. They gave their names as Ed Smith and Charles E. McDonald. It didn't take long to identify Smith as George Frankhauser. Questioning by detectives proved fruitless.

Thomas Riley gave the reporters an interview. "Although I am not commonly known as a detective, I have done a little work along those lines, and when I get interested in a case I will take my hat off to no one. I became suspicious of these men when they began to spend money so freely. The next step was to see that they didn't get away. They attended to that part of it by themselves by inviting me to go traveling with them. I think the evidence against them is strong. It will be hard for them to explain how come they have so much money. But they fit the descriptions exactly."

Riley was wrong. Frankhauser fit the description almost perfectly. McDonald was 5'9 1/2", 155 pounds, forty-three years old, dark hair and light brown eyes. The original description of the taller bandit was 5'11", 180 pounds and slightly stooped shoulders. McDonald was muscular and erect. McDonald was the bandit who fired his revolver from the cliff not the taller one who entered the express car.

Sheriff O'Connell was notified of the capture and arrangements were made to extradite the pair to Montana. Sheriff O'Connell and deputies arrived in Spokane and the bandits were brought into the jail office. Sheriff O'Connell introduced himself and proceeded to place waist chains with handcuffs and leg irons on the pair. The bandits realized what was happening and yelled for a lawyer, extradition papers and God's help, not necessarily in that order. The fight was brief as the bandits were outnumbered. With restraints in place, the party departed to cross Idaho and enter Montana sans legal papers. They were locked in the Flathead County Jail at Kalispell.

The prisoners were a constant source of trouble. Fearing an escape, the sheriff took the cell keys and hid them. One evening a frightful uproar was heard so the sheriff and jailers rushed into the cell block to see McDonald beating the hell out of a fellow prisoner Ed Sergeant. Sergeant's face looked like bloody hamburger. McDonald was ordered to stop but he refused. Strategically placing his deputies, the sheriff entered the cell and jailer Bellflour locked the door behind him. At this point McDonald quit to rush by the sheriff only to face a locked door and a cocked Colt revolver. Sullenly he returned to his cell. The sheriff started a constant watch on the pair. One Friday afternoon a jailer saw a cut bar in McDonald's cell. Instead of moving McDonald to another cell and repairing the cut bar, an armed guard was placed by a window to constantly watch McDonald. There were no more escape attempts in Kalispell.

George Frankhauser was born to Albert and Mary Frankhauser in Springfield, Pennsylvania, in 1872. He had been convicted of stealing liquor out of boxcars near Kalispell in 1898. He had escaped twice from the storeroom where he was held, once going twenty-two miles wearing an "Oregon boot." (The boot consisted of a heavy iron ring that was locked around one ankle and rested upon another iron band, which was supported by braces attached to the heel of the wearer's boot. The weights varied according to the wearer's size or likelihood of escape. It was invented and patented by Oregon State Prison Warden J. C. Gardner.) A new jail had since been built. He was sent to the Montana State Prison at Deer Lodge on October 10, 1898, with his crime partner Tom Clancy. They were the best of friends and inseparable. They walked the yard together planning a train robbery. Through cold winters and hot summers they planned and planned. Clancy was 5'10 3/4", blue eyes, 180 pounds, forty-three years old in 1907, slightly stooping shoulders and dark hair. Clancy was released on January 1, 1906. Frankhauser was

Montana State Prison at Deer Lodge. The brick cell block was built in 1912.
Photo: Norman Davis

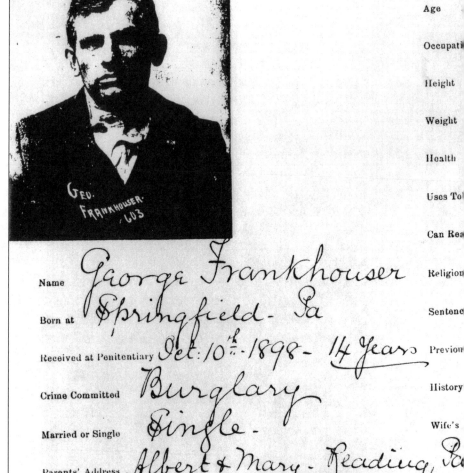

	Age
	Occupati
	Height
	Weight
	Health
	Uses To
	Can Rea

Name George Frankhouser

Born at Springfield - Pa

Received at Penitentiary Oct: 10th - 1898 - 14 Years

Crime Committed Burglary

Married or Single Single -

Parents' Address Albert & Mary - Reading, Pa

Brothers' ~~and Sisters'~~ Address Clarence & Harry - Read

Marks & Scars Scar on top of right foot, exten

Small round scar back of le

History of ~~Crime~~ 2 Small round blue marks ba

	Religion
	Sentenc
	Previou
	History
	Wife's

borer

6

6*

-od

rite Yes.

Hathead County   Size Shoes # 7.

tions ✓

lease ✓ Life sentence at Leavenworth U.S.P.

✓

g. Pa:-
g from little toe to joint of big toe from Seal
wrist; - Small Scar end of left thumb:-
f each thumb. —

is: January 10th 1907. Exp: of Sent—

Nose

Mouth Teeth, 2 Upper front and Several back gone

Chin Cheeks, long. —

Ears

Features Small.

Complexion Light

Hair & Beard, light

Carriage

Photo N

Age

Occupa[tion]

Height

Weight

Health

Uses T[obacco]

Can Re[ad]

Religio[n]

Senten[ce]

Previou[s]

Histor[y]

Wife's

Name *Thomas Clancy*

Born at *La Crosse - Wis:-*

Received at Penitentiary *Oct: 10th: 1898- 12 Years.*

Crime Committed *Grand Larceny:*

Married or Single *Single*

Parents' Address *Mother Mrs. H. V. Day #2033 M*

Brothers' and Sisters' Address

Marks & Scars *2 Scars on back of Neck;- one*

History of Crime

1

...broader

' 10³⁄₄ "

74⁸

...ood

Write _Yes_

...Flathead County

...tions

...elease

...son St: - St Louis

3 cornered Scar over left Eye. ———

...is. Jan⸍ 1ˢᵗ. 1906.   Exp: of Sent.

Eyes _Blue._

Nose

Mouth Teeth. 2 lower & 2 upper front gone, back good

Chin

Ears

Features _Large & Coarse._

Complexion _Dark._

Hair _Dark._

Carriage _Beard, Sandy._

Size Shoes #8½.

Montana State Prison cell block, a standard pattern of most prisons. The prison was closed years ago, but self-guided tours are available for a small admission fee.

Photo: Norman Davis

released January 19, 1907. Clancy was the other robber. He was never identified or caught.

Lawmen could not get McDonald to talk about himself. They suspected that he had been tried on a burglary charge in Utah the previous year but was not convicted. However, his crime partner was.

Sheriff O'Connell was cooperative when the district attorney wanted to move Frankhauser and McDonald to the Lewis and Clark County Jail in Helena so they could be tried in Federal Court.

In July the Montana legislature authorized creating Lincoln County out of the northwest corner of Kalispell County. Elections were scheduled, but at the time of the robbery, Lincoln County existed only on paper. There was no money to operate, or even a proposed budget. There were no necessary officials, such as a district attorney, sheriff, judge or clerks, etc.

The trial could have been conducted in Kalispell, but there was not enough money available. The state of Montana could hold it in Helena, but the costs might bankrupt the state treasury.

To pay for the witnesses' travel, food and lodging from Chicago, Minneapolis/St. Paul, Moorhead, Spokane and various other places would require an enormous sum. It was wisely decided that the federal government would conduct the most expensive trial in Montana's history. This was all legal as there was U.S. mail stolen. It was advantageous also because the penalty was far more severe for mail robbery. This meant the federal government could plea bargain a lighter sentence in exchange for the returning stolen money. Money talks, but it only says one word—goodbye. So on January 4, 1908, they were moved to Helena.

Arriving in the jail they were thoroughly searched and a hacksaw blade was found in McDonald's undershirt. Several other blades were secreted in his rectum and were not found. They were placed in the most secure cells available and separated by a steel door. They were forbidden to speak to one another. So they communicated by tapping their cups on the steel bars in Morse code. Twice a day they were let out of their cells to use the wash basin and toilet, empty their slops and refill their water bucket. Twice a week they were shaved by the barber. On the seventh of January their Bertillion measurements were taken. Sheriff Shoemaker asked McDonald if he had any distinguishing marks on his body. McDonald said no. Then the sheriff rolled up McDonald's right shirt sleeve exposing a tattoo PM, however another source says TM.

Sheriff Shoemaker said, "P means Charles and M means McDonald I suppose?"

McDonald answered, "No you fool, it means midnight."

A reporter present said of him that he appeared to be of more than ordinary intelligence, carried himself well, was erect and muscular. Green was present in his light brown eyes—inscrutable, well set in his head, they were the most distinguishing thing about him. When in repose they were lusterless, but when he spoke they lighted up. He could pass in any crowd as a prosperous attorney or business man.

It was time to plea bargain. However, between railroad detectives, U.S. Marshall Merrifield, insurance agents and Sheriff Shoemaker and U.S. attorneys with conflicting egos, there was

Lewis and Clark County Jail, southeast corner at Ewing and Breckenridge streets, Helena, Montana, circa 1916. The window through which Frankhauser and McDonald cut the bars and woven wire screen and escaped is in the rear opposite the nearest arched entrance. The rooming house window of Miss Bessie Hawkins is clearly visible. The rooming house has been converted to apartments.

Photo: Montana Historical Society, Helena

Lewis and Clark County Jail remodeled to the Myrna Loy Theater at it appeared in 1994.   *Photo: Montana Historical Society, Helena*

Dougal "Duke" McGregor, deputy and day jailer, circa 1916.

utter chaos. Sheriff Shoemaker finally had Frank Conley, warden of Montana State Prison talk to Frankhauser, as he knew him well. Frankhauser said if they received a sentence of less than twelve years they would return the money, identify their partner and testify against him. Both convicts had a great fear of a life sentence in Leavenworth. Shoemaker allied with detectives, and with Frankhauser's map they went to Bonners Ferry. The money was buried in a stone crock by the Northside School. Shoemaker and detectives found the school and a stone crock by a hole in the ground. Both were empty.

Returning to Helena, Shoemaker was informed that the remainder of the stolen money had been found by Fritz Lang. He was the watchman at Sylvanite and he read old newspapers in his remote cabin. He saw pictures of McDonald and Frankhauser identified as train robbers and remembered their visit. He searched the Chickadee Mine and sure enough under a pile of rocks was the money, $14,000. He notified the authorities and was rewarded with a finder's fee of $2,000. This was reported in local papers but denied by the railroad detectives and insurance people. Sheriff Shoemaker told the bandits no deal as the money was under six feet of snow. Maybe in the spring when the snow was gone they would talk about it.

With ominous and foreboding feelings about a bleak future, the pair strengthened their resolve to escape. The sheriff loaded a shotgun with number 8 birdshot and told jailers if they thought or even suspected the two might escape they were to shoot both in their cells. The sheriff added a night guard to patrol outside the jail at night till 6 A.M.

The railroad paid the wages of the guard Henry Hay. Thus, not being totally loyal to the sheriff, Hay altered his schedule to suit himself. He liked to enter the Bon Ton Cafe at 5:30 A.M. when it opened and enjoy a piece of pie and a coffee. Then he would take the 6 A.M. streetcar home and build a fire to take the chill out of the air and go to bed. Mr. Lemkie, the night jailer also liked to have breakfast at the Bon Ton and rode the 6 A.M. street-car home. Thus there was no jailer on duty till Duke McGregor arrived at 6 A.M. This opportunity was too good for the bandits to pass up.

Miss Bessie Hawkins lived in one of the rear rooms of Schaffer Flats at 18 North Rodney Street. It was her custom to lower her window blinds in the evening to insure the privacy of a proper maiden lady. It was also her custom to raise the blinds in the morning to observe weather conditions so she might dress appropriately for her walk to work at Butchers and Fowlers Dry Good Store. On Saturday morning March 21, 1908, at 7:20 A.M. she raised the blinds and saw two men exit a barred window at the rear of the jail and run south. She quickly went to the dining room and told Mr. Sanborn, the landlord, what she had seen. He walked slowly and cautiously to the jail office. He told Duke McGregor, the day jailer, what Bessie had seen. McGregor went to the basement and verified the presence of the trustees. (Trustees were inmates who enjoyed a lot of freedom in doing the necessary chores in a jail. They cooked, cleaned, painted, etc.,

132

and even groomed the sheriff's horses across the street.) He then went to the cells that housed McDonald and Frankhauser and saw a cut bar on the floor. Frankhauser and McDonald's cells were empty. What he said shouldn't be repeated.

Other witnesses saw the pair run up Dry Gulch a quarter-mile from the jail. Henry Hay was called in from a sound sleep to join the posse. In thirty minutes the posse was mounted and started to search Dry Gulch. The gulch was brushy with a lot of trees and prospect holes on steep hillsides. The posse searched all day long and twice came very close to the bandits' hiding place. After dark the bandits watched Henry Hay and Ray Clements eat supper at Andy Holm's ranch. Later the pair sneaked back into Helena and checked into a rooming house. They cleaned up and brushed their clothing. McDonald then went to a saloon and exchanged thoughts with his fellow drinkers about the jail break. They stayed in Helena about two weeks then took the train to Fargo, North Dakota.

Their trial had been scheduled to start the following Monday, March 23. Witnesses had been subpoenaed from Chicago, St. Paul, Spokane, Bonners Ferry, Butte and Kalispell. All were housed in hotel rooms at taxpayer expense. They were held till Thursday and then sent home. Even the hobo Umbray was released. He had enjoyed his stay, caught up on his washing and mending and even gained a few pounds.

Obviously rumors started that the escapees had inside and outside help. An investigation was ordered by the U.S. attorney general; Alvin McNish, U.S. attorney, started asking questions. His report filed in September was one long narrative of gross incompetence and employee disloyalty and supervisorial neglect. The jailers had orders to search the cells twice a day but didn't. Frankhauser had cut a hacksaw frame from his cell chair. This was very obvious even at a glance. There was no one on duty from 5:30 A.M. till 6 A.M. in the jail. With the hacksaws found, it took four minutes to cut a cell bar. There was one cut bar in their cell door, one cut bar in the corridor grill, one cut bar in the rear window plus the wire mesh window screen was cut. Most of the openings were only about eight inches wide but both bandits squeezed through to freedom (perhaps the thought of life in Leavenworth encouraged them). But the question remained, where did they get the hacksaws?

Thomas Ford and his nephew James Young were interviewed at Deer Lodge. Both had been awaiting trial in Flathead County when Frankhauser and McDonald were there. They swore in affidavits that they saw attorney Thomas Long give three hacksaw blades to McDonald in exchange for a map to find a stone crock full of money near Northside School in Bonners Ferry. (Many local people did not believe Ford or Young belonged in prison. Landon T. "Andy" Carter was Thomas Ford's nephew by marriage. Carter's wife [Ford's niece] had died recently of natural causes. Carter got drunk, to assuage his grief, and made threats that he would kill Ford, his son Jack and Young on sight, then kill himself. Carter got a rifle and went to Ford's place. Carter made noise at the gate and Ford and Young investigated only to be shot at by Carter. Ford then kicked and choked Carter to death. Young stood by doing nothing. The governor of Montana granted them clemency and they were released in 1908.)

Frankhauser and McDonald realized they couldn't stay in Montana. They couldn't trust anyone because of the reward offered. What they didn't know was that the reward was canceled when they were apprehended and not reinstated when they escaped. U.S. Marshall A. W. "Will" Merrifield was a long and trusted friend of President Theodore Roosevelt. That is why Roosevelt appointed Merrifield as marshall in the fall of 1906. He was a cattleman, not an experienced lawman. Merrifield did not print and distribute reward posters on the wanted men. Even as late as 1910 the U.S. postal inspectors did not have an accurate description of the escapees.

Frankhauser arrived in Fargo and soon recruited Joe Velthause and his common-law wife Birdie Anderson as crime partners. An illiterate day laborer, John McCarthy was invited to join the gang so that they could hide stolen goods in his barn. The three men went to work on the Great Northern and the Northern Pacific Railroads, but not for wages. Two would break into boxcars and throw boxes of merchandise out on the dirt road. The third man drove a team and wagon on the road picking up the boxes. The three then sold the stolen goods. They drank and gambled in the saloons in Fargo, Crookston and Grand Forks.

Clay County Sheriff Archie Whaley was told by discreet informants that Frank Wolf, Jack McCarthy and Joe Velthause were responsible for the rash of boxcar thefts. The sheriff shared this information with Barnesville Police Chief Forsythe. Forsythe said he knew the responsibles by sight and would arrest them. On November 28, 1907, Thanksgiving Day, he and his officers Will Wright and John Sieber, foregoing a bountiful feast, drove out to McCarthy's farm. As they approached the house, two men jumped out the rear window and ran. For two miles they ran till they fell exhausted on the ground gasping for air. They were returned to Barnesville and jailed. Joe Velthause started talking as soon as he was handcuffed. He confessed to several thefts and informed on his crime partners. Frank Wolf kept quiet. Birdie Anderson was having dinner in Fargo across the state line. A deceptive phone call lured her across into Minnesota and she was arrested on the Red River Bridge. Two weeks later Jack McCarthy was arrested, but Dr. Alexander and saloon owner Pete Engels immediately posted his $1,000 bail.

McCarthy remained free till his trial in November of 1909. He was a well-known and liked local pioneer, having settled there in 1883. He had married Tillie Smith in 1898. Frank Wolf's Bertillion measurements were sent to St. Paul. On December 23, Bertillion expert James Murname sent a telegram to Sheriff Whaley informing him that Frank Wolf was actually George Frankhauser, wanted for train robbery and escape. The wheels of justice started to turn.

George Frankhauser also got busy. However, a jail informant seeking favor sent a note to the sheriff telling of Frankhauser's plans for escape. Released prisoner Joe LeMere, nicknamed "the Jap Frenchman," having completed his sentence for vagrancy, was escorted to the edge of town. There he was told not to return. Ignoring these instructions, he bought magazines and hid hacksaw blades in their bindings. Then he returned to the jail and asked that the magazines be given to prisoners to read. Less than twenty-four hours after being released, he celebrated New Years Eve of 1909 in his former cell. His stupidity and generosity cost him another thirty days.

On New Years Day, Marshall Merrifield arrived in Moorhead from Helena. Two reporters and deputies witnessed the interview with Frankhauser. Frankhauser was sullen, he had lost weight and he had grown a beard. He denied his identity. Merrifield had Frankhauser remove his false teeth plate. It matched the Bertillion description and Frankhauser admitted his true name. He agreed to return to Montana without an extradition fight if it was similar to his previous extradition fight.

The Great Northern Railroad had a reputation of not paying rewards that they often offered. Sheriff Whaley and Chief Forsythe asked the Attorney General of Minnesota to look after their interests in securing the reward before releasing Frankhauser to Marshall Merrifield. The AG assured them of his assistance.

The long-delayed trial was started on January 20 of 1909, in Helena. Half a dozen witnesses testified that Frankhauser was at the crime scene. The money taken from him and McDonald in Spokane still had the bank bands of the Commercial Bank of Chicago around the small stacks. Pearl Raymond, one of the girl-friends, told of her involvement with the pair in Butte. No one missed a word of the sordid affair. The drinking marathons in Butte and Bonners Ferry were described in detail. This somewhat embarrassed Frankhauser, but otherwise he was unemotional. Because of the move from state courts to federal jurisdiction his previous attorney Long (also a state senator) had resigned. Two capable attorneys, S. A. Balliet and Anton Horsky, represented the defendant, but the evidence was overwhelming and unim-peachable. The case was given to the jury at 3:35 P.M. on the January 26. At 6 P.M. Frankhauser was chatting with the newly elected Sheriff Higgins in the marshall's office. The verdict was guilty. The next morning Judge Hunt sentenced him to life in Leavenworth.

Nonchalantly, Frankhauser told the sheriff, "it's sixty days and a hundred-dollar fine." In commenting, Frankhauser was minimizing his long-dreaded sentence. He was not the tough guy he attempted to be. Cautious and alert, Marshall Merrifield and two deputies escorted Frankhauser to the dreaded federal prison in Kansas. He did not say one thing to identify his third partner or where McDonald was.

Will Merrifield made a judgment call. Since there was no reward offered for McDonald why spend money on printing and distributing wanted posters? Lawmen would have little or no incentive to search for a dangerous fugitive. At that point in time, if a lawman was injured and recovering he was off the payroll. If killed in the line of duty, the only compensation was the generosity of contemporaries as they passed the hat. However, some were dedicated regardless.

On April 6, 1910, Frankhauser sawed out of his cell in Leavenworth. Guard Wheeler caught him in the corridor just a short distance from his cell. Frankhauser had a pair of shears, knife and a rope made of overalls in his possession. He was then confined in solitary. Then on April 17 a few miles east of Benicia, California, Southern Pacific's *China Japan Fast Mail* train was robbed of $500. Two and possibly three men were involved. The Leavenworth newspaper immediately reported that McDonald had furnished Frankhauser with the hacksaw and plans were to rob the train together. McDonald was reported captured in a cabin near Martinez, California, and identified as McDonald. There is little truth here. McDonald did not furnish the hacksaw to his former crime partner and he was not arrested. James Franklin and Fred Hansen were arrested for the train robbery, but the train crew could not positively identify them. They filed a writ of *Habeas Corpus*, which means "Bring me the body." A judge hearing the writ released them for lack of evidence on April 30. They were not rearrested. Neither man resembled McDonald.

In October of 1910 the U.S. Postmaster General requested from Will Merrifield a detailed description of McDonald. Merrifield replied that a description was printed in the April 21, 1908, edition of the *Anaconda Standard*. Actually it was the 22nd. Then a Montana newspaper reported that McDonald had been arrested in Baugh, New Mexico, by Postal Inspector Earl

137

Smith of the Denver office. Baugh, New Mexico, does not nor did it ever exist—more yellow journalism.

As time went slowly by Frankhauser became melancholy and attempted suicide. He was housed near a young Robert Stroud, later to become the Birdman of Leavenworth. (He was not allowed birds as pets or patients during his seventeen years at Alcatraz.) Frankhauser became friends with Jeff Spurlock, an Arizona train robber. George Frankhauser, prison number 6298, died February 9, 1921. Cause of death was recorded as peritonitis-exhaustion following intestinal obstruction. He was forty-eight years old.

Joe Velthause was sentenced to one year in the Minnesota State Prison at Stillwater. John McCarthy was sentenced to ten months and served the minimum time as they both turned state's evidence.

On March 10, 1910, Judge Taylor in Moorhead, Minnesota, handed down his decision in favor of the plaintiffs seeking the reward that had been offered by the railroad. There were an eastern group and a western group. Sheriff Whaley of the eastern group was awarded 45 percent. The western group, headed by Jesse Howe, received 55 percent of $5,000. They appealed and the reward was raised to $7,000. However, the railroad contended that the crime occurred in Montana and the bandits were captured in Washington and they weren't listening to a Minnesota judge. Judge Taylor decreed that Sheriff Whaley could seize railroad property and sell $7,000 of it. Legal fees by this time almost equaled the reward.

Tom Clancy was never identified as the third bandit. Perhaps he took his share of the loot and went his way. He might also have drowned when the raft foundered or caught pneumonia as a result of being wet and cold and died in the forest.

Charles E. McDonald, if that was his real name, was never apprehended. He might have returned to retrieve the loot only to learn it had been returned to its rightful owners. If he was drinking at the time and got into an ugly mood he might have burned Sylvanite and cut the phone line. There weren't any windows to break in that wilderness.

Epilogue—Historical Notes

Libby Dam was built on the Kootenai River forming Lake Koocanusa which flooded Rondo Siding.

The Great Northern Railroad is now part of the Burlington Northern Railroad.

Lewis and Clark County Jail in Helena was replaced by a modern one in the 1980s. It had been seriously damaged by an earthquake in 1935 but was repaired. In the late 1980s it was extensively remodeled and is now the Myrna Loy Theater.

Located on "the richest hill on earth," Butte was a fabulously wealthy mining town. It has been in decline for many decades. The ABC Saloon location is now a vacant lot.

The Casey Hotel is gone and the lot is vacant.

Riley's Dance Hall still exists but is closed. The sign boasts "Since 1895."

George Frankhauser feared that he would not live to parole. He gave a map to the hidden loot to his friend Jeff Spurlock. Spurlock was released in 1925 and searched for the money for seven years. When a cache of money and bonds were found near Bearmouth he told of his search to a reporter in 1932. Obviously it was not the Rondo Siding loot. It is strange that Frankhauser thought that both Clancy and McDonald would not return for the money. It is possible that he knew both were dead. It is also possible that he insured Spurlock's trust and friendship with a worthless piece of paper.

James Sharkey was obviously involved but backed out of the actual robbery. He was a career criminal who served time in McNeil Island Federal Prison, Oregon State Prison and Montana State Prison (two terms) under various names. His last reported crime was burglary of a Billings department store in 1932. He stole women's stockings and served ten months.

Pursuant to mandating a recent popular vote Bonners Ferry, Idaho, closed all saloons on Saturday, August 27, 1910, at midnight. C. B. Emery, proprietor of the State Bar shipped his fixtures to Spokane and left for the coast. Jack Nave, owner of The Club spent $500 remodeling his building, offered it for rent and left for Mexico. Arvid Peterson who operated The Court Bar relocated in Montana. James Fitzpatrick, proprietor of the Casey Bar, devoted his time operating a butcher shop. Do you suppose that the good people of Bonners Ferry were expecting the train robbers to return for a drink?

References

Barnesville Record and Review, Barnesville, MN
Coeur D'Alene Press, Coeur D'Alene, ID
Kailspell Journal, Kalispell, MT
Montana State Archives, Helena, MT
Montana State Historical Society, Helena, MT
Moorhead Weekly News, Moorhead, MN
Mt. Montana Daily Record, Helena, MT
Northern Idaho News, Sandpoint, ID
Oregon State Archives, Salem, OR
Rocky Mountain Husbandman, Helena, MT
Spokane Spokesman Review, Spokane, WA
The Troy Hearld, Troy, MT
The Cascade Courier, Helena, MT
The Anaconda Standard, Anaconda, MT
The Butte Miner, Butte, MT
The Bonners Ferry Hearld, Bonners Ferry, ID
The Fargo Forum and Daily Republican, Fargo, ND
US Regional Archives, Seattle WA
Washington State Archives, Olympia, WA

Journal of a Country Lawyer
Crime, Sin and Damn Good Fun
E. C. (Ted) Burton
5½ x 8½, 240 pp. SC
ISBN 0-88839-364-4

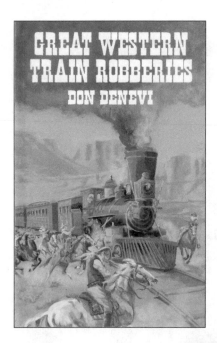

**Great Western
Train Robberies**
Don Denevi
ISBN 0-88839-287-7
5½ x 8½, SC
208 pp.

**Jack Mould and the
Curse of Gold**
Elizabeth Hawkins
ISBN 0-88839-281-8
5½ x 8½, SC
176 pp.

MORE GREAT HANCOCK HOUSE TITLES

History

Cariboo Gold Rush Story
Donald Waite
ISBN 0-88839-202-8

The Craigmont Story
Murphy Shewchuck
ISBN 0-88839-980-4

Curse of Gold
Elizabeth Hawkins
ISBN 0-88839-281-8

Early History of Port Moody
Dorathea M. Norton
ISBN 0-88839-197-8

End of Custer
Dale T. Schoenberger
ISBN 0-88839-288-5

Exploring the Outdoors
Eberts & Grass
ISBN 0-88839-989-8

Guide to Gold Panning
Bill Barlee
ISBN 0-88839-986-3

Guide to Similkameen Treasure
Bill Barlee
ISBN 0-88839-990-1

Gold Creeks & Ghost Towns
Bill Barlee
ISBN 0-88839-988-X

Gold! Gold!
Joseph Petralia
ISBN 0-88839-118-8

Logging in B.C.
Ed Gould
ISBN 0-919654-44-4

Lost Mines and Historic Treasures
Bill Barlee
ISBN 0-88839-992-8

The Mackenzie Yesterday
Alfred Aquilina
ISBN 0-88839-083-1

Pacific Northwest History
Edward Nuffield
ISBN 0-88839-271-0

Pioneering Aviation of the West
Lloyd M. Bungey
ISBN 0-88839-271-0

Yukon Places & Names
R. Coutts
ISBN 0-88839-082-2

Northern Biographies

Alaska Calls
Virginia Neely
ISBN 0-88839-970-7

Bootlegger's Lady
Sager & Frye
ISBN 0-88839-976-6

Bush Flying
Robert Grant
ISBN 0-88839-350-4

Chilcotin Diary
Will D. Jenkins Sr.
ISBN 0-88839-409-8

Crazy Cooks and Gold Miners
Joyce Yardley
ISBN 0-88839-294-X

MORE GREAT HANCOCK HOUSE TITLES

Descent into Madness
Vernon Frolick
ISBN 0-88839-300-8

Fogswamp: Life with Swans
Turner & McVeigh
ISBN 0-88839-104-8

Gang Ranch: Real Story
Judy Alsager
ISBN 0-88839-275-3

Journal of Country Lawyer
Ted Burton
ISBN 0-88839-364-4

Lady Rancher
Gertrude Roger
ISBN 0-88839-099-8

Ralph Edwards
Ed Gould
ISBN 0-88839-100-5

Ruffles on my Longjohns
Isabel Edwards
ISBN 0-88839-102-1

Where Mountains Touch Heaven
Ena Kingsnorth Powell
ISBN 0-88839-365-2

Wings of the North
Dick Turner
ISBN 0-88839-060-2

Yukon Lady
Hugh McLean
ISBN 0-88839-186-2

Yukoners
Harry Gordon-Cooper
ISBN 0-88839-232-X

Outdoor Titles

12 Basic Skills of Flyfishing
Ted Peck & Ed Rychkun
ISBN 0-88839-392-X

Adventure with Eagles
David Hancock
ISBN 0-88839-217-6

Alpine Wildflowers
Ted Underhill
ISBN 0-88839-975-8

Birds of North America
David Hancock
ISBN 0-88839-220-6

Eastern Mushrooms
Barrie Kavasch
ISBN 0-88839-091-2

Guide to Collecting Wild Herbs
Julie Gomez
ISBN 0-88839-390-3

Northeastern Wild Edibles
Barrie Kavasch
ISBN 0-88839-090-4

Orchids of North America
Dr. William Petrie
ISBN 0-88839-089-0

Roadside Wildflowers NW
Ted Underhill
ISBN 0-88839-108-0

Sagebrush Wildflowers
Ted Underhill
ISBN 0-88839-171-4

Tidepool & Reef
Rick Harbo
ISBN 0-88839-039-4